Y0-BZL-837

Develop
Confidence

Develop
Confidence

Build a positive
approach to
life and work

ROS TAYLOR

DK

LONDON, NEW YORK,
MUNICH, MELBOURNE, DELHI

Produced for Dorling Kindersley
by **terry jeavons**&**company**

Project Editor — Sophie Collins
Project Art Editor — Terry Jeavons
Designer — Andrew Milne
Picture Researcher — Sarah Hopper

Senior Editor — Simon Tuite
Senior Art Editor — Sara Robin
Editor — Elizabeth Watson
DTP Designer — Traci Salter
Production Controller — Stuart Masheter

Executive Managing Editor — Adèle Hayward
Managing Art Editor — Karla Jennings

Art Director — Peter Luff
Publisher — Corinne Roberts

Special Photography — Adrian Turner

First American Edition, 2007
Published in the United States by
DK Publishing, 375 Hudson Street,
New York, NY 10014

07 08 09 10   10 9 8 7 6 5 4 3 2 1

ISBN 978-0-75662-608-2

ED246

DK books are available at special discounts for bulk
purchases for sales promotions, premiums, fund-raising, or
educational use. For details, contact: DK Publishing Special
Markets, 375 Hudson Street, New York, NY 10014 or
SpecialSales@dk.com
Printed and bound in China by Leo Paper Group

Contents

Introduction

Confidence is the key to leading a successful and happy life—you can't function well without it, and you need it to help you in every area. Good confidence levels make decision-making easier, and smooth the way in making friends, building relationships, and helping you maintain a successful profile at work.

But you can't buy confidence, and just the consciousness that you are lacking in it can make things worse instead of better. So what should you do? Develop Confidence helps you assess the areas in which your confidence is low—or missing altogether—and offers you practical ways to build it up and make it work for you. It covers inner confidence, how to make a good first impression, how to become more confident in relationships and work, and, above all, having successfully

developed confidence, how to guard it and begin your journey toward a naturally confident future. Each of the five chapters offers case studies, tips, and simple techniques you can practice, every one of which is

dedicated to heightening your awareness of how
you behave, and the ways in which both you and others can
work toward increasing rather than diminishing or eroding
your confidence.

Confidence is also a key
element in motivation. A
motivated person has
impact and creates a

> **Confidence feeds itself—
> as you develop it, it
> will start to grow of its
> own accord**

memorable first impression; they will also be more stimulating
company and influence others easily. You will find that as your
motivation grows, your life will improve and you will get more
of what you want—and the more successful the pattern of
your life becomes, the more confident you will feel. To
become truly confident, you may need to change, so get rid
of the thoughts in your head that deny change. Sometimes, if
your thinking has been with you for years and has become
habitual, it may feel fixed and immutable: remember that your
thinking style can change along with everything else, and you
can replace it with optimistic and positive patterns of thought.
Use this book effectively and, as your confidence increases,
you will learn to be bold—and a bold approach to life will
ensure that you are successful and happy in your ventures.

Assessing Your Skills

Answer these questions honestly to assess your confidence now—they will help you become aware of the areas that need work, and may also give you some insights about the people who will help you the most. As you answer, think about the different areas of your life, and how having more confidence will help you in each of them. Do the exercise once before reading the book and again when you have completed it to see how you have progressed.

	Before	After

1 Walking into a crowded room for the first time, how do you feel?

Before: B

A Intimidated—I feel everyone is looking at me.
B Nervous—I look around for someone I know.
C Stimulated—there are a lot of people here I'd like to talk to.

2 If you have a socially challenging situation coming up, how do you think of it?

Before: B

A I try to prepare for the worst by thinking of everything that might go wrong.
B I try not to think of it at all—it will only make me more nervous.
C I make a plan for dealing with it to make me less nervous.

3 You are asked to speak to 50 people at a department meeting; what's your reaction?

Before: B

A I do everything I can think of to get out of doing it.
B I buy some time by saying that I will think about it.
C I agree immediately, and begin to plan my talk.

	Before	After

4 **A close friend is critical of your behavior—what do you do?**

A I get angry—they're my friend, they should be on my side.

B I thank them for their advice, but feel resentful.

C I think about whether the criticism is justified, and if I should act on it.

5 **It's your birthday and you're going out, but your partner has opted not to change first. How do you respond?**

A I accept them as they are, and say nothing.

B I accept them as they are; who am I to judge?

C I suggest they change—it is a special night.

6 **You arrive at a costume party to find that everyone else is in evening clothes. What do you do?**

A I go straight home, feeling humiliated.

B I stay, but feel self-conscious all night.

C I accept that it doesn't really matter, and enjoy being different.

7 **You attend an interview for a senior post within your company, but your colleague is given the job. How do you feel?**

A Embarrassed—why did I feel that I could do the job?

B Defensive—it discourages me from trying again.

C Curious—I'd like to know why, so that I will be successful next time.

8 **If you are socializing in a group, which person are you?**

A I'm the one who talks to the people I know, but tends to avoid new people.

B I usually listen until I find there's a conversation I can join in with.

C I like to be the center of the group, and I try to get everyone to join in.

9 **A first date went well, but after three days, they haven't called. What will you do?**   *C*

A Nothing—I'd be embarrassed if they didn't want to see me again.
B I'd call and ask why they hadn't called me.
C I'd call and suggest a second date—but one in a group situation.

10 **You need to make an important decision— how do you approach it?**   *C*

A I worry about it for a few days, then decide rapidly at the last minute.
B I ask various people if they think my decision will be the right one.
C I solicit various opinions, then make my mind up.

11 **A friend butts in as you are talking to someone you find attractive. Do you:**   *C*

A Stand back from the conversation.
B Take them to one side and ask what they think they are doing.
C Take back the conversation gracefully, involving all three of you.

12 **You have a life goal for the remote future; what do you do to make sure it happens?**   *C*

A I continue as I am; there's no point thinking about anything that far ahead.
B I think about it regularly, but I haven't taken any action yet.
C I've worked out how to get there, and I check my progress regularly.

Final Scores

	A	**B**	**C**
Before		*L*	*L*
After			

Analysis
Mostly As

Not only do you lack confidence, but you know it, and you tend to avoid challenges. You tend to see things as "just happening" to you, rather than believing you can take control of situations and change the outcome in your favor. You need to become less afraid of action, and to understand that dreams will remain only dreams unless you devote some energy and self-belief to making them happen. You need to start small and build your confidence gradually, but in measurable steps.

Mostly Bs

Your lack of confidence is not overt, but your inner confidence needs shoring up. You tend to procrastinate on decisions, and you often hide your true feelings under a veneer of decisiveness, but this masks the fact that you don't always feel as confident as your behavior indicates. You need to work on developing a sense of self-worth so that you can stay calm when problems or tough situations arise, and respond from a confidence based on your own self-knowledge of what is right for you.

Mostly Cs

You don't lack confidence in most situations, but you may find that thinking around situations more than you currently do will offer you more varied opportunities and challenges in life. Because you think most things through carefully and are a good planner, you need to ensure that there is still space for spontaneity. A closer look at how you operate, and at when you feel at your most confident, may help your life to become more stimulating and surprising.

Conclusion

After you have answered the questionnaire for the first time, look at the answers carefully and note any areas that you feel need work. Read the book, practice the exercises, tips, and techniques as you go, and make sure you notice the effects of the various actions you take as you take them. When you have completed the book and practiced all the techniques, retake the questionnaire—you should find that you give fewer A answers and have a better balance of B's and C's.

First
Impressions

The first impression you make is the most important of all. People who are meeting you for the first time will base their thoughts about you on the way you look, your body language, and the way in which you meet their eye and greet them. It takes much less time than you might think to create a positive impact. This chapter will show you:

- How to create a good first impression
- How to assess your body language
- How to improve it
- How to understand the body language of others
- How to make the most of yourself
- How to relax with your newfound confidence

Create Instant Impact

You have up to 30 seconds to make a good first impression and just five to make a bad one. Remember, people will assess you visually, basing their decision on your appearance, clothes, gestures, and body language.

Make a Positive Impression

It seems rather brutal that you have so little time, but it is true. You might like to think that people take their time to get to know the inner person before delivering a judgment, or at least that they should. But life does not work that way. You need to make your impact with your overall look—and a first meeting really is a "brief encounter." Think of the last time you met someone new and how quickly you formed an opinion of them. Experiment next time you are introduced to a new contact.

First impressions are the most lasting

Time how long it takes you to make your mind up about them. If you reacted negatively at first, but then changed your mind, how did they influence you?

Test Yourself

There are many different ways in which you can assess your confidence rating. Imagine a scale ranging from 10 for maximum confidence to 0 for minimum, and place yourself on that scale. To become more aware of what contributes to your confidence rating, ask yourself the following questions:

• Which situations make me feel particularly confident?
• Which situations undermine my confidence?

When you have the answers to the questions, you have the key to knowing what it would take to improve your rating. Keep this key at the back of your mind. Ask a friend to help by gauging your self-assessment as you begin reading this book and after you have completed it.

Practice Selling Yourself

Try thinking of yourself as a product you want to market and sell. Make a mental 30-second commercial about yourself. If you can take an objective view, you may find you are more "salable" to other people than you realized.

Outline your talents, personal attributes, skills, and unique selling points. Think yourself into the part of salesperson with a huge amount of enthusiasm for your product. You will need to get the pitch and the packaging exactly right, or you may not perform like the fast-selling consumer product you want to be.

→ What was your core message?

→ Did you deliver your pitch in short, punchy, upbeat sentences?

→ Did any minus points, apologetic tones, or self-criticisms creep into your commercial?

→ Have you used each of the 30 seconds usefully, or did you waffle for some of the time?

→ Will your presentation make people remember you, realize they need or like you, or want to hire you?

Self-Presentation

HIGH IMPACT	NEGATIVE IMPACT
• Being aware of, and confident in, your special qualities	• Indulging in negative thoughts about yourself
• Thinking in terms of making the most of what you have to offer, and working to develop it	• Making a unilateral decision that what you have to offer is not good enough
• Inviting feedback, and listening to it with an open mind	• Treating feedback as criticism and ignoring or resenting it

TIP **A lifetime's impression takes no more than a moment's input, so make sure you put in the necessary effort in advance.**

Learning Body Language

Nonverbal communication is crucial to effective, positive impact. Be aware of how you look when you speak. Check not only your own body language, but that of others. Learn to speak and understand body talk.

Discover Nonverbal Communication

A classic theory for the effectiveness of spoken communication was developed by the eminent psychologist Albert Mehrabian. Illustrated by the chart below, it states that just 7 percent of effective communication is verbal—conveyed by the words we say—whereas 38 percent is vocal—derived from the way we say those words, our voice, tone, and inflection. Nonverbal communication, though, scores highest of all, at 55 percent—expressed by our body "language."

Watch What Is Being Said

People transmit large amounts of information through eye, facial, and chest movements. It has been estimated that the average person speaks for only 12 minutes a day; the rest of what is being "said" is expressed by gesture. It has been found possible for a trained observer to tell from their gestures alone what language a subject is speaking, without hearing the words.

Human Messages

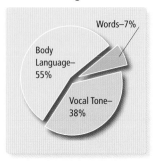

Words–7%

Body Language–55%

Vocal Tone–38%

Your Body Has a Language As this pie chart shows, surprisingly little of what we call "language" is expressed by the spoken word.

TIP **Remember that eye contact is a powerful tool used by confident people. It can maintain, deny, command, or yield communication.**

Introducing Body Talk

Test yourself to see how many of these nonverbal cues you can interpret. Bear in mind that there are no definitive "right" answers: you are looking at the nuances of posture.

Look at the different body language of the examples. See how many you can work out before you look at the suggested range of answers. Practicing looking at other people's stance and gesture will help you widen your own body-talk vocabulary, and will also make you a more effective and fluent communicator in interviews, presentations, or social encounters. You will be learn to be able to read a huge range of signs, although interpretation depends on nuance and context—the "phrasing" of body language.

Interpretation

A Thinking, pondering, considering. Upturned face, eye contact cut off.

B Expressing big emotion—feeling joy, or under threat.

C Relaxed or casual. Confident hand-on-hip stance, perky and irreverent.

D Furtive, caught in the act. Head turned around, back hunched, and knees bent.

E Welcoming with open, giving gesture. Arms extended in potential embrace.

F Coy, flirtatious. Face turned down, eye contact cut off.

G Menacing, angry, exasperated. Big gestures for strong feeling.

H Bashful, shy, holding back. Hunching of shoulders appears unconfident.

Improve Your Body Language

Now that you have understood the importance of seeing and interpreting other people's body language, it's time to tackle your own. Remember, you are both the message and the messenger.

Stand Confidently

Your posture is a key part of the message you convey when meeting people. Confident people have open, secure body language; they stand upright yet relaxed, hands open, engaging in calm eye contact. This stance is good for your confidence—but it benefits your body organs, too. They are not compressed by tension, and find it easier to perform their natural tasks. A passive stance is one where the person stands with shoulders hunched and body closed, avoiding eye contact. Organs are squashed and have to work harder to do their job, taking up extra energy. An aggressive stance can include clenched fists, glaring eyes, tapping feet, and rigid jaw and upper body. The message conveyed is negative and the impact on the self equally damaging. Even if you aren't feeling confident, adopting a confident stance will help you to feel in control of a situation.

5 minute FIX

In a situation in which you don't feel confident, give yourself this quick positive posture talk to help you stand confidently:

- I am a puppet and the puppeteer is giving me a gentle pull on the strings on my shoulders and head.
- I look confident and interested, I feel confident and interesting.

Look Outward

Your face is one of the most expressive parts of your body. It reveals a great deal about you and is likely to be the first point of visual contact between you and another person. However, you may not be aware of your own expressions and of the different, potentially misleading messages they can convey. When you look at yourself in the mirror, you may see quite a neutral face, but that is because you know

what you are feeling inside. What others see is often more expressive and full of emotion than you intend, and thus open to potential misinterpretation. For example, the tension an anxious person shows on entering a room full of strangers could be mistaken for irritation, disapproval, or a lack of interest—people will make their own interpretations and will not approach you if they feel your reaction may be unwelcoming or confrontational. It is important to be aware of what your face says, and have the ability to make your expression open to approach.

CASE study: Effective Role-Playing

Yasim, a middle manager in a software company, was eager to be promoted, but he kept being turned down for positions for which, on paper, he was ideally qualified. After his third failure, Yasim decided he needed to look at his interview technique. He began to wonder if his body language might be to blame, and asked his girlfriend, Sara, to perform a role-play interview with him and then give him feedback on how he came across. They interviewed each other, filming the event and swapping roles. Yasim was astonished to see his body language in action.

• He realized that the way he leaned back, legs outstretched, making slightly confrontational eye contact, gave the impression that he was uninterested in the interview, or even challenging.
• Yasim learned that unpracticed, unrehearsed body language can convey the opposite message from the one intended.
• In his next interview, Yasim ensured that his body language expressed his enthusiasm, leaning forward and engaging in calm eye contact with the interviewer. He was offered the promotion on the spot.

Learn the Power of Your Eyes

The eyes are often the most attractive features in a face—not necessarily their color, size, shape, or embellishment, but simply their gaze and its directness. The nature of your eye contact with others, how direct and intense it is, depends on the relationship with the person with whom you're exchanging it—its closeness (physical and emotional), and the emotion being conveyed. A direct stare can indicate intense feelings of an amorous, hostile, or fearful kind, whereas a deflected gaze is linked with shyness, superiority, or submissiveness.

Engage with Your Surroundings

If you lack confidence, you may find that your eyes drop to the floor as you enter a room. If you feel as if all eyes are upon you, you hide your embarrassment by looking away. This sort of body language actually makes you appear aloof. Shy people typically say that they feel that they look uninteresting, but it is more likely that their body language is conveying a lack of interest in their surroundings. The way forward is to engage with your surroundings openly, thus inviting other people to approach you.

TECHNIQUES *to practice*

Shyness most often hits when you enter a meeting room or gathering for the first time.

Try this exercise for a quick confidence boost when you feel shyness overcoming you:

1 As people register your entrance, make visual contact with each glance, and smile. Hold the smile a moment, then glance away.

2 Sit or stand with your back to the wall and imagine what is happening in front of you as a play unfolding before you.

3 Look alert and stimulated. People will be drawn by your apparent confidence and interest.

Recognize Different Glances

Look closely at people absorbed in conversation and watch their gaze pattern. Eye contact will be made and lost as the gaze is juggled between the two parties. If you become skilled at observing and correctly interpreting the messages of eye contact, it will help you to be a more sensitive and effective communicator.

Eye Contact Resumed
As a speaker begins to talk, she glances at the listeners to check the effect of her words.

Contact Deflected
A glance away may indicate a gaze "break" before a participant re-engages in the talk.

Contact Held
This listener watches the speaker closely, looking intently, ready to pick up the conversation.

TIP **Practice your fluency in glances by watching other people's conversations. Notice the gaze pattern of the speaker commanding the greatest attention.**

Simple Steps to Confidence

Build your body language tips into a routine which you can slip into automatically in any socially or professionally challenging situation. You don't have to work through all the points every time, but each one will help you to become more confident, as well as to appear so.

→ Smile. Not only does this send a positive message to others, but smiling releases endorphins to the brain to provide energy, dynamism, and a feel-good factor about yourself.
→ Walk tall, head erect, to convey high self-esteem.
→ Look everyone in the eye and listen carefully, nodding and responding to what they are saying.
→ Open up your body language to encourage people to talk to you. Crossed arms create an unwelcoming barrier.

Assume Confident Body Language

You can start to use confident body language before you feel fully confident inside. Straighten your back, look calmly and directly at the person you are talking to, and walk tall. You will appear confident already. A relaxed smile strongly reinforces the effect. Think of these simple strategies as the signature outfits in your new confidence wardrobe: strategies that will work for you over and over again. Good habits take exactly as long to acquire as bad ones—if you consciously change your body language for three weeks, in another nine you will find that the new language has become a habit. The more you turn your attitude and interest outward, toward other people, the less self-absorbed and self-conscious you will feel. You will be surprised by how quickly assumed interest in others becomes real interest, as you listen and become engaged with what they have to say.

Use Gestures Well

Gestures are, in many ways, just as powerful as speech. Think about how you use them, as well as when and where. The use, type, frequency, and meaning of hand movements vary between contexts and countries. Make sure that you are using the right gesture for the situation you are in, and do some research if you work with people from other cultures, or travel a lot, to ensure that your gestures mean what you intend them to mean. People can be suspicious of those who use gestures lavishly, but they are crucial in everyday communication. If you have ever given directions to someone who does not speak your language fluently, you will know how effective they can be when expressing concepts. Unconscious gestures, such as fiddling with a shirt cuff or piece of jewelry before an interview, or tapping your foot while trying to look fascinated, can also betray your inner feelings when you don't want them to show. Become conscious of how much your face and body can convey without uttering a single word.

Use the Cycle of Confidence

As you enter a room, assume a confident stance; look up and out

⬇

When people turn to look at you, smile and meet their gaze like someone who is already confident

⬇

The less confident will gravitate toward you, hoping that your confidence will mask their shyness

⬇

Seeing you at the center of a group, the more confident will move toward you to see what is of interest

Be Confident in Your Looks

How you look affects the way you feel. A lack of confidence in your appearance may make you behave defensively, and it is often this, rather than your actual appearance, that can have negative consequences.

Project a Confident Appearance

The way you dress and how you look may convey the wrong impression both to others and to yourself. Stand in front of the mirror in casual clothes—for example, your old jeans—and write down what that image conveys. Then put on your dressiest clothes—perhaps the suit you use for interviews—and jot down the message you are giving out. Is the image you thought you were projecting the one you see in the mirror? Do you feel different—more, or less, confident—when you wear your suit? You need to be alert to the impact of the image you are conveying at the moment and the one you want to present to others in the future. Having worked on your inner confidence, now it's time to enjoy an outer makeover.

Context Dictates Suitability
Which of these two interviewees is more appropriately dressed depends on the job they are applying for.

Making Your Clothes Work for You

HIGH IMPACT

- Buying clothes that suit your body shape and lifestyle, accentuating your best features
- Wearing clothes you buy yourself to make your own image statement
- Checking your wardrobe, and researching what suits you before you buy
- Adding color to your choice of clothes, for a bright and confident appearance

NEGATIVE IMPACT

- Buying clothes that are fashionable but not suitable for your body shape
- Wearing clothes other people have bought for you: the image decision is theirs, not yours.
- Buying expensive clothes in haste without considering what you actually need
- Wearing bland colors, giving the impression that your image of yourself is also bland

Find Your Style

To "dress for success" you need to find a style that suits you, your lifestyle, and your professional or daily context. A good way to start would be to ask the advice of a personal shopper in a department store (increasing numbers of men as well as women are calling on their skills). You will get ideas about what suits your body shape and coloring. Get advice from a number of personal shoppers and buy at the best price. Image consultants will charge for their advice, but it is worth investing in an independent, professional opinion if it prevents you from making expensive mistakes. Get advice on your hair and grooming, too. Being well groomed will make you feel and appear more confident. Watch some of the many makeover shows on television for extra tips, and don't be too shy or too proud to ask people whose style you admire for advice.

Clothes don't make the man...but they go a long way toward making a businessman.

Thomas Watson Senior

Relaxing with Confidence

Now that you have discovered and begun to develop your confidence, it's time to learn how to relax, to protect and maintain it when you are feeling stressed. Relaxation techniques are among your most useful tools.

Take Time Out

As you make the journey to the new, confident you, you will need to make a few pit stops along the way to rest, recuperate, recharge, and restore. What you need to imagine and then create is a comfortable space, a haven where you can relax and restore your energy and calm when things get very busy, or when you feel your confidence is vulnerable. Even when your schedule is hectic, remember that it only takes a minute to recharge your batteries, enabling them, and you, to run effectively for longer.

A varied pace of activity is the most productive

Create a Haven

Find a quiet corner in your room, or your office building, in which you can be assured of a few minutes of solitude and peace. Try to make this a regular spot to go to, and even if sometimes you just sit there quietly, you will begin to feel the benefits. Imagine it as a space for "me time." You will find that your mind and body will become relaxed once you reach your haven, because of its association rather than its physical location. Turn your cell phone off before you do anything else. You are only taking a few minutes out of your day. It's time to learn how to be still, and concentrate just on breathing, slowing and calmly.

TIP **To remain focused during a busy working day, teach yourself to relax—you should spend five minutes refocusing for every two hours of work.**

TECHNIQUES *to practice*

When you need to energize yourself fast, use this exercise in breathing.

Known as the Power Minute, it will help you to focus your mind fast and to concentrate on any important task you need to begin.

1 Check the number of breaths you take in a minute, counting in and out as "one."

2 If you are taking more than 12, your breathing is too rapid and your breaths too shallow. You are not breathing out enough carbon dioxide.

3 Repeat the minute, concentrating on breathing in and out more slowly. Aim for a count of less than 10. If you are still breathing too fast, repeat.

Remember, effective exhaling benefits the whole body—it rids the lungs of stale air and relaxes the muscles.

Learn Deeper Relaxation

The Power Minute exercise is effective as a quick fix, but if you have a little more time, try this short routine for a deeper, longer-lasting body and brain refresher.

- Sit on a chair, your right hand hanging by your side, your left hand resting on your left thigh.
- Close your eyes and breathe in slowly, counting to six, then hold for a count of two and breathe out for a count of four.
- Breathe with your diaphragm and concentrate on the image of blood flowing from the heart, down your right arm, turning at the fingertips, going back up the arm, and then continuing around the body. Continue to breathe slowly.
- Focus on the fingertips of your right hand, and you will become aware of a slight tingling in the tips. As you relax, this tingling will get stronger.

Open your eyes after a couple of minutes. You will feel refreshed and ready to engage with the rest of your day.

Inner 2
Confidence

This chapter focuses on that intangible quality of inner confidence or self-esteem. Personal, difficult to define, sometimes fleeting and elusive, it forms the foundation of our successful development, both personal and professional. Learn to understand how your own thought processes can propel you toward your goals. This chapter will show you how to:

- Believe in yourself
- Identify and combat confidence sappers
- Pinpoint your own pessimistic thinking and convert it into optimistic thinking
- Develop positive coping strategies
- Externalize, visualize, and then realize your goal

Beat Confidence Sappers

First, ask yourself why you lack confidence. Do the people or situations around you sap your self-esteem? Potential sappers include partners, family members, colleagues, peer groups, friends, and children.

Your Family Influences You

Research has shown that the family you were born into does make a difference. The eminent psychologist Gordon Claridge conducted major research into the relative influences of upbringing over genetics, or nurture versus nature. His results showed that if one or both parents lack confidence, their children have between a 60 and an 80 percent chance of lacking it, too. Although genetics may have a profound influence, that still leaves between 40 and 20 percent leeway for external influences to play a part.

Confidence can be created as well as inherited

Outside Relationships Influence You

If a child is made to feel a failure by his or her school and/or peer group, the damaging effects can last a lifetime. Generally speaking, many of our views and beliefs will have been carved out at school or formed in the family context at a particularly impressionable age. As an adult, you must confront any negative thoughts that undermine your confidence. Relationships, personal or professional, in which you feel trapped and helpless will sap your self-esteem. It is important to be aware of, and protect against, the damaging effect of negative interaction in relationships. In a professional context, managers do not always encourage their employees to have the confidence to speak up about ideas or disagree with decisions. A desire for conformity on the part of an organization often demotivates employees and makes them feel starved of the oxygen of self-expression, and diminished as a result.

Act to Keep Your Confidence

Read through this list of people and mentally check any who might be undermining you. Remember how they have interacted with you, and what effect that interaction had.

Consider in each case whether they bring out the best in you and support your confidence, or deflate you and steal your energy.

→ Mother   → Boyfriend/partner   → Teacher/professor
→ Father   → Girlfriend/partner   → Work manager
→ Brother   → Children   → Colleagues
→ Sister   → Close friend   → Neighbors

When you have gone through the list, make a mental note to see more of the people who build your self esteem. Conversely, if there is someone who saps it, limit your exposure to them.

Dare to Express Yourself

Speaking up about what you believe and what you want is essential to your well-being. The greatest threat to your equilibrium is the suppression of your natural feelings and needs, so it is important that you learn to ask for what you want. In a major survey into confidence carried out in Britain, 81 percent of the people who responded had never asked for promotion, and 51 percent had never asked for a pay raise. They failed to speak up because they had no confidence that their wishes would be granted, but in reality, over three-quarters of those who did speak up were given the pay raise or the promotion they wanted.

TIP **Be aware of the negative impact some people and situations can have on your self-esteem. Learn to seek out confidence supporters and suppliers instead.**

Take Control

Learn to spot and handle situations or people with the potential to sap your confidence. Identifying how they work will make it easier. If you have experienced some of the following feelings with people close to you, then you may well have been "sapped":

- You felt good about yourself until meeting this person, but shortly afterward you were unaccountably depressed. This sort of sapper can often adopt a paternal or maternal attitude toward you, but their power comes from their ability to control you. You may only feel supported by them when you are upset or needy, thereby enabling them to feel in charge.

- You feel drained after meeting someone because of their exhausting one-upmanship. They are deeply insecure and "winning" is the means by which they feel better. Refuse to engage in a competition with them—indulging in this sort of competitiveness will only make you feel insecure yourself.

TECHNIQUES
to practice

Once you know that someone is sapping your confidence, take action in one or more of the following ways:

1 Limit contact so that you are less in their company.

2 Plan to spend more time with people who make you feel good about yourself.

3 Ask the sapper directly to be more positive and/or supportive of you.

4 Respond to any internal dwindling of confidence with an extra-positive and energetic attitude.

5 Refute any criticism openly.

6 Ask the sapper if they are feeling well—say that you have noticed they are being more negative than usual.

7 Refuse to dwell on their behavior, even in your quieter, more reflective moments.

Defend Your Self-Esteem with a Smile Deflect confidence sappers by taking criticism or negative comments with a smile. Ask yourself if there is anything you can learn from the criticism—if you are positive there is not, dismiss it.

Defend Yourself

If your self-esteem has been diminished by a person's comments, whether directly or indirectly, they are undermining you. It may make them feel better if they disparage you, but this is no reason to allow them to knock your confidence. Defend and protect yourself from unwarranted criticism. Distraction interferes with any negative thinking in your head. Coupled with activity, it will change the biochemistry of the brain, releasing endorphins and helping you to feel better. An alternative method is to think through the criticism, and ask yourself what you would think if it was directed at someone else.

TIP Activity is the enemy of introspection. If you are feeling negative, take some exercise and remember—you are in charge of your thoughts.

Work toward Optimism

Confidence starts on the inside and is greatly influenced by how you think. Discover ways of thinking that can help to propel you toward a more confident future and divert you from the pitfalls of pessimism.

Think Positive

After extensive research into thinking styles, psychologists established the ways in which they are associated with success and positive outcomes. Sadly, many people do not have optimistic thoughts. They may feel that life has intervened to deal them a bad hand. In fact, research reveals that events, even horrific ones, do not affect people as much as family influences. You tend to take on thoughts and beliefs similar to those you were brought up with, unless you consciously make an effort to change them. The following pages show you some of the pitfalls that can lead to patterns of pessimistic thinking. Identify yours, then read the antidote. You will discover a more optimistic approach.

"Always" Thinking

When bad things happen, you believe that they are perpetual and permanent. You are more likely to give up easily on life and to feel

5 minute FIX

An imaginary filter is effective when you urgently need to turn a negative thought into a positive one, fast.

- In your mind, put a filter over your thoughts.

- Negative thoughts don't get through the filter; it discards any but positive thoughts.

- When negative thoughts are denied to you, you will find that your creativity will supply you with a positive alternative.

Believing you can climb the mountain takes you halfway up it already in your mind; believing you can't means you will never leave base camp.

John Foster

Move toward "Sometimes" Thinking

You can turn "always" thinking to "sometimes" thinking very easily by voicing your thought and then modifying it. This is particularly effective when you are aiming an "always" thought at someone else.

"ALWAYS" STATEMENTS	"SOMETIMES" STATEMENTS
"You never do what I want."	"I know you act independently, but it's good if sometimes you do what I want."
"Diets never work."	"Diets don't work for me when I am tired. When I relax, dieting will be more effective."
"I'm always in such a mess."	"I'm in a mess now, but I will pull myself together soon."

more helpless in the face of a crisis. This "always" thinking means that you believe that life will deliver blows no matter what you do. When you see yourself as a martyr to fate, it engenders passivity and discourages you from taking positive action to solve problems. How do you counteract it? When you feel you are in danger of entering a vicious cycle of "always" thinking, tell yourself that nothing is forever. Don't listen to the "always voice" in your head. Switch it off—it doesn't deserve your time.

"Sometimes" Thinking

On the other hand, if you believe that a bad event is just a temporary setback, you will bounce back and regain your optimism. This is "sometimes" thinking: you are merely suffering a temporary setback and will be back on track soon. Using more optimistic thinking, you are more relaxed— and therefore more creative—when it comes to thinking of ways to get out of bad situations. "Sometimes" thinking gives you the energy to realize that situations change, that problems can be solved, and that you have the power both to change and to solve them. Listen to the "sometimes voice"—it is positive and gives you space.

Diminish "Everywhere" Thinking

"Everywhere" thinking involves believing that when one thing happens, it will generalize to every area of your life. A single setback prompts you to overreact: you see your future as catastrophic, and your life as completely ruined by this one negative occurrence. As a result, you are more likely to succumb to depression. The language in which you describe events can be illuminating. If you use words like "disaster," "failure," "awful," or "disgusting" a lot, your subconscious reacts by becoming stressed. If you continue to think and speak in this way, in no time, even as little as three weeks, it becomes a habit. Examples of "everywhere" thinking when bad things happen are

- I've lost my job; I'm a complete failure.
- That relationship is over; I am utterly unattractive to the opposite sex.
- That policy is nonsensical; the government is a total waste of time.

Find the Positive Answer

It is much more effective to believe that you have been unsuccessful only in a specific area than to extend your thoughts in negative directions until you have persuaded yourself that you are a complete failure at everything you attempt. Sticking to specifics means that you can chip away at a particular issue and turn it around, but if you generalize, it is more likely that you will get stuck in a rut and believe that you can't change. Limit the areas in which you lack confidence, and ring-fence and protect the others in which you already believe that you can succeed. Avoid the domino effect of "everywhere" thinking by saying to yourself instead:

- I won't be unemployed forever; there are other jobs in the field that I can apply for.
- That relationship didn't work out, but someone else will find me attractive.
- While I disagree with some of the government's policies, others have something to offer.

Build Something Positive

However negative an event, something positive can nearly always be extracted from it if you are prepared and able to make the effort to think constructively and objectively.

When something bad happens, you can't always control the fallout from it. If it's a situation in which you had an acting role— a promotion you failed to achieve at work, for example— then there is usually a tendency to self-blame or to blame somebody else: your boss or the interviewer, perhaps, or even the colleague who was given the promotion instead of you. Instead of descending into a spiral of negativity, step outside the situation and try thinking in a different way. Ask yourself:

• How would you feel if you hadn't applied for the promotion?
• If you were outside the situation, and unconnected to it, would you still feel negatively toward any of those people?
• Who does that negativity harm—them, or you?

Having concluded that negative feelings harm only yourself, you should be able to move into a more positive mind-set.

Objectivity Helps You cannot control who wins the game, but it need not spoil your all-around enjoyment of the sport.

J. DiMauro

Thinking Styles

OPTIMISTS SAY
- "It might not be just me."
- "Now I need to do something about it."
- "I can sort this out."

PESSIMISTS SAY
- "I am to blame completely."
- "There's nothing I can do about it."
- "It's all hopeless; I'm a failure."

"Me" Thinking

"Me" thinking means that, when bad things happen, you automatically blame yourself. You may internalize anything that goes wrong when, realistically, the blame should be directed elsewhere. Low self-esteem quickly follows. A point here about the differences between men and women: women tend to blame themselves for everything that goes wrong, while men tend to blame everyone but themselves. Some examples of "me" thinking are:

- It's all my fault.
- I let the team down.
- I'm to blame for the failure of my marriage. I just wasn't interesting enough.

"Not Me" Thinking

When you find yourself using "me" thinking, the opposite, "not me," may work, but is not always appropriate. Ask yourself if someone else might be to blame, or if the situation arose through a combination of events. Women especially should entertain the possibility that they are not to blame. For those who lack confidence, even asking the question is a step forward. However, to blame others without any introspection or careful judgment may not be appropriate. So "not me" thinking must be used judiciously. The equivalent "not me" thoughts to match the "me" thinking examples given above would be:

- It might be someone else's fault. I must find out.
- The team could have helped me out more.
- My partner contributed to the failure, too.

> **The optimist proclaims that we live in the best of all possible worlds; and the pessimist fears this is true.**
>
> James Branch Cabell

Acknowledge Success

When good things happen, the "me" thinker is willing to admit that they were successful and that the successful outcome was attributable to their efforts in this instance. The "not me" thinker believes that they deserve to win. And of course there is nothing wrong with that, provided that when things go wrong they admit their errors and learn from mistakes.

Your Inner Critic

When something goes wrong, optimists engage in positive "sometimes" thinking, accompanied by appropriate action. They focus solely on the specific event and consider externalizing the blame. On the other hand, pessimists, when faced with adverse events, will employ "always" thinking, internalizing the blame and applying it to much more than the specific event.

think SMART

If, despite your efforts, your wish to turn your negative spiral into a positive one isn't working, think laterally to banish the negative forces from your mind.

Usually the best way to deal with negative thoughts is to banish them firmly. If this is not proving effective, though, try the opposite approach: welcome them. Turn your thinking around by acknowledging them mentally, thank them for alerting you to the problems they highlight, and tell them that they have fulfilled their function. A formal acknowledgement of your negative feelings may distance you from them.

Externalize Your Concerns

Over time, you become so accustomed to your thoughts that they play like a commentary in your head. If they tell you that you are a failure, their impact is damaging. To reduce their effect, you need a reality check

Write Things Down

Externalizing is a process whereby you verify your thoughts and check them against reality. The more you are able to externalize, the more confident you will become. Always keep a pen and paper by your bedside. If your mind is going around in circles when you wake at 3 a.m., try writing down all the issues that are keeping you awake. You can then decide which ones you realistically will be able to solve, and which you will have to let go. There is something therapeutic about seeing your negative thoughts or fears on paper. Once you have externalized them, it minimizes their effect, and they become instantly more manageable. By committing them to paper, you are taking the first step toward solving them.

Use Your Support System Make sure that you get the help you need to stay confident with a reliable network of friends and professional contacts.

Start a Secret Service Group

Identify a group of friends or professional helpers, ideally between six and eight people (with this many, you'll almost always be able to reach one or two of them), whom you can trust to give you honest feedback. This is your "Secret Service" group. You can call on them in tricky situations—for example, if you want to leave your job, or take serious action against someone. Access to a range of disinterested views will help you to crystallize your own.

Value External Views

View these people as insiders giving you outsiders' views. They are close to you, but not to the situation, dilemma, or personalities involved. Write your secret service list alongside their numbers in your planner, or program it separately into your cell phone. This will guarantee you fast access to advice and encourage you to use your friends and advisors more regularly.

TIP Solicit a range of views when you are dealing with a problem—other people's ideas will augment your own, as well as supporting them.

CASE study: Facing Your Fears

Kylie, an opera singer, always feared forgetting her words. She would have nightmares about it, was sick before every performance, and lost a lot of weight. She realized that if she was to continue in her profession, she would have to tackle these fears. She wrote her consequences down, working her way through them: if she forgot her words, the audience would think she was a fool, and she would never be asked to sing again. This would mean that she could not have a career in singing and would have to find something else to do.

• *As soon as Kylie realized that she had sufficient resources within herself to find an alternative career if she really had to, she relaxed. She learned that facing your fears is always better than hiding from them, and, as the worry disappeared, she started to enjoy her professional work much more.*

• *She had taught herself to cope with adversity by turning a hypothetical worst case into a real-life best-case scenario. The ghosts of her imagined nightmare had been thoroughly laid to rest.*

Move toward the "So What?" Answer

Anxiety and worry tend to undermine confidence—you fear the worst in any situation, or are always expecting some calamity to happen. If you often find yourself saying things like "But what if it doesn't work?", "What if I go there and I don't know anyone?", "What if I ask a question and look foolish?", or "What if I go for promotion and don't get it?", you need to play the game of consequences.

Look beyond the Barrier

Think of your worst fear or embarrassment, then imagine that it has already happened. Using the process on the opposite page, take yourself through all the possible consequences that could come to pass. Pursue your "what if" thinking to its natural conclusion. Face the fear and see if it is as bad as you had imagined. When you carry out this exercise, you force yourself to confront the worst possible

TIP Try playing consequences with a friend: eliminating your fears together will help you realize how unfounded many of them are.

scenario, and will find that you are able to put the problem into better perspective. When you have practiced the game of consequences with a number of differing scenarios, skip the in-between stages and head straight for the "so what?" conclusion. This is a sign of growing confidence— it indicates that your more carefree mind-set has become a habit—and it should be your ultimate goal. Everyone feels fear: it's a natural emotion faced with a difficult situation. But if it is strong enough to hold you back from taking a course of action, or fulfilling your dreams and ambitions, you need to tackle it head on. "So what?" doesn't mean that you don't care what happens—only that you know that nothing can stop you trying to go for your goals.

Play the Game of Consequences

Choose your worst fear or embarrassment. Mentally, put it in the blank space left for it below, then work your way through the stages.

→ What if................ happened? What would be the consequence?

→ Then, if that happened, what would be the result?

→ And the consequence of that would be?

→ And what further consequences could that have?

→ The final consequence of that would be?

Eventually, at the end of this succession of events yet to occur, you will find that you reach the point at which you are able to say "so what?", face your fears, and move on.

Winning Visualizations

Visualization is a powerful technique used by psychologists to help people overcome phobias. If you visualize or imagine a feared situation in advance, you will be better prepared to cope with the real thing.

Visualize, Minimize, and Realize

Even though your worry may rank several levels below a phobia—it could simply be about carrying out a challenging task, for example—the technique can be effective in these situations, too. Visualizing a way of dealing with the worry, imagining each stage of the event, or revisiting a nightmare can all help to give you more control over your thought patterns and bring you additional confidence in dealing with those situations with which you are uncomfortable.

TECHNIQUES *to* practice

When you are faced with something to worry about, put it out of your mind with a particular image.
Perhaps you are worried about giving a presentation to a large crowd? Try this technique:

- Imagine that a large janitor's brush is calmly sweeping aside the fluttering leaves that represent your anxiety.
- Say to yourself "I will worry about that the day before the presentation."
- When that day comes, mentally sweep aside the leaves and say, "I will worry about that in the hour before the presentation."
- When the hour of the presentation arrives, sweep again, telling yourself to worry about it afterward—by which time it will be too late to worry about it at all!

Choose an image that works for you. It does not have to be a brush; it can be any implement that will dislodge your worry, but it is important that the "sweeping" movement is calm and soothing.

Learn to See Yourself as a Winner If you are used to putting yourself down mentally, you may find it hard at first, but it's essential for your future success that you become a winner in your own eyes.

Practice Mentally

Two groups of soccer players were asked to improve their goal-scoring capabilities. The first group went onto the field and practiced kicking the ball into the goal for three hours. The second group was asked to visualize kicking the ball into the goal mouth for the same amount of time. They did not practice on the field. When both teams competed at the end of the exercise, the team that visualized goal-scoring scored more goals. The reason? The second team had no failures. They scored each time in their imaginations and entered the competition with confidence. Their experience had been wholly positive.

TIP **Find a quiet corner to practice your visualization. Engage your creative imagination to create a vivid and positive picture for yourself.**

Keep a Mental Diary

When you are in a situation in which everything is new and challenging—for example, just after you have started a new job—begin each day by summoning some personal reinforcement. Sit on the edge of the bed and imagine success at every point in the next few hours. You could say something like, "My new colleagues want to listen to me, the morning has been a success, and the next meeting holds no fear. They like what I am telling them, and now it is lunchtime, so half the day has gone and I am feeling confident and relaxed." You will find that any feelings of dread disappear as you visualize success and simultaneously help yourself to relax.

> **Remember that what we dread in our minds rarely comes to pass**

Help Yourself to Positive Dreams

When you are experiencing serious problems, you may find that your anxiety emerges in your dreams. At night, your mind will play you movies of awful situations: falling off cliffs, being trapped in burning buildings, or crashing cars.

To confront this, change your dreams.
→ If you are falling, imagine that you have grown wings.
→ If your car is headed for a crash, imagine that you can accelerate fast enough to escape.
→ Program yourself just before you fall asleep with the additional, positive scenario in your dream.

Your solution does not have to be rational; it just needs to get you out of your dream situation. Just as fear can penetrate your unconscious, so positive thoughts can redress it.

Watch Your Thoughts

HIGH IMPACT

- Behaving as though you believe in your own success
- Choosing to remember past successes in all areas of your life
- Being conscious of your underlying thoughts at all times

NEGATIVE IMPACT

- Fearing failure that hasn't yet happened
- Selectively remembering only situations that defeated you
- Allowing your unguarded thoughts to undermine you

Control Your Breathing

Controlling your breathing can also help coordinate your mind and your body. Try this simple breathing exercise. First exhale all your breath, then breathe in and mentally count to "four successes" (one success, two successes etc.). Hold your breath for four successes and exhale for a further two, building up to four as you practice more. Do it for just a few minutes when you feel anxious or fearful of a new challenge. If a memory of a bad experience in the past threatens to color your thinking and your view of the future, try the breathing exercise to relax. Make it part of a daily routine. Adapt these suggestions to your own routine and schedule and you will find they become powerful tools in your confidence-boosting resource.

Chant Your Way to Confidence

When the Reverend Jesse Jackson was trying to instill a sense of self-worth into a group of African Americans at one of his gatherings, he asked them to chant "I am somebody" over and over again until they believed it. If your self-esteem ever lets you down completely, use the same chant. Add to it, if you want—you might say, "I am somebody worthy of respect," "I am somebody who is a winner," or "I am somebody who is worth knowing." Chant it at least three times, like a mantra, every morning until you start to believe it.

Summary: Gaining Confidence

Inner confidence or self-esteem is fundamental to our successful development, both personally and professionally. Use this summary to help you throw off the shackles of low self-esteem and negative thinking, and to build the inner confidence to voice and achieve your goals.

Work Your Way to Confidence

1 Combat Confidence Sappers → **2 Turn Negative to Positive Thinking**

1 Combat Confidence Sappers

Identify those personal and professional relationships and situations that sap your self-esteem

↓

Act positively by spending more time with people who bring out the best in you, and boost your confidence

↓

Ask for what you want instead of allowing your natural feelings and needs to be ignored

↓

Combat "sappers" by taking control of their source of power—don't compete with those trying to "beat" you

2 Turn Negative to Positive Thinking

Turn "always" thinking into "sometimes" thinking by voicing your negative thought and modifying it

↓

Nip "everywhere" thinking in the bud by refusing to allow one setback to infect every aspect of your life

↓

Avoid "me" thinking— blaming yourself for everything that goes wrong—when others might also be to blame

↓

Think constructively and objectively by finding something positive in even the most serious setback

3 Learn to Externalize Your Concerns

Reduce the effect of your negative thoughts by externalizing them, checking them against reality

Write down your negative thoughts and fears, then use the scaling technique to reduce their impact

Seek advice and encouragement from friends and advisors who are close to you but not to the problem

Play Consequences with your fears until you are able to say "so what?", face your fears, and move on

4 Visualize, Then Realize Your Goal

Visualize the problem in advance so that you can cope with the real situation if it happens

Control your worries by mentally "sweeping" them aside until after the event

Use the power of imagination to visualize a positive outcome to a problem

Endpoint
Remember, what you dread the most rarely comes to pass in real life

Confidence
and
Relationships

3

The effect of confidence across the relationship spectrum is broad—it affects all aspects of relationships: how to find, maintain, and commit to one, cope with one that is fraying at the edges, and the way in which a relationship ends. This chapter will teach you about:

- Emotions and how we experience them
- Relationships and how they come about
- Gaining confidence in dating
- Influencing skills with the opposite sex
- Maintaining relationships
- Coping with the end of a relationship

Emotion

Relationships are about connections and emotions—not just love and warmth, but frustration, boredom, and anger, too. How well you deal with emotion will inevitably reflect your ability to handle relationships.

Learn Your Emotional Style

Emotional expression works best when it is appropriate to a particular context: tears aren't suitable in an important meeting, for example, nor is icy control when you're meeting a much-loved friend after a long break. Everyone has a different emotional style. The four main types are listed below. Think about your own style and which of these describes it best:

- **Avoidance** You do all you can to avoid powerful emotions. You do feel, and strongly, but the strength of your emotions means that you feel foolish and out of control. Instead, you say nothing, hiding behind politeness in the hope that these disruptive feelings will

CASE study: Reconciling Emotional Styles

Joshua and Eva's six-month relationship ran smoothly until a close mutual friend suddenly died. This event was their first stressful experience as a couple. Joshua's response was to withdraw emotionally, while Eva was openly upset and needed constantly to discuss her feelings. She confided in her sister that she found Joshua's emotional denial undermining, believing it meant he did not love her enough to confide in her. Her sister suggested that she discuss it with Joshua unemotionally, without using language that seemed to lay blame on either party.

- *The discussion revealed to Eva that Joshua, far from being cold, was frightened to share the depth of his feelings.*
- *Joshua learned that Eva was strong enough to support him, and that he could open his emotional self to her. The couple accepted that there is no "right" way to express emotion.*

> **A man who has not passed through the inferno of his passions has never overcome them.**
>
> Carl Gustav Jung

go away. Many people would do almost anything rather than experience an uncomfortable emotion. And, by the same token, they hate being on the receiving end of unbridled feeling—their only response is to placate at any cost. As a result, they may miss out on some of the greater joys and more intense experiences of life.

- **Denial** You deny experiencing any emotion whatsoever. This ensures that you can keep your cool through both good times and bad. Sometimes it is easier to pretend that you don't actually feel anything. You may be dissociating yourself from strong feeling because facing it would mean making profound changes in your life.

- **Catharsis** You simply rid yourself of any pent-up emotion. When angry, you let rip—it's over in minutes and you feel much better afterward. There are some people who use emotion as a way of releasing tension.

Experiment with Emotional Style

If you are facing a problem, work through the different styles and see how each would affect your behavior.

Avoidance
You remain at the perimeter of the problem, unable to get to grips with it

Denial
You study the problem rationally, but cannot solve it without emotional engagement

Catharsis
You find that the problem makes you angry. The problem remains unsolved

Directness
Your emotional literacy guides you when analyzing the problem. You use both emotion and analysis to solve the problem

If they vent that tension on the football field, or crying at a sad movie, this can work for them. However, if their emotion tends to express itself in rages, or manipulative behavior with those close to them, it can damage their relationships irretrievably. Venting emotion without considering the consequences may make you feel better in the short term, but in the long term it creates more problems than it solves.

- **Directness** When you feel strong emotion, you know you must act on it. You recognize its significance, acknowledge it, and change your circumstances to accommodate it. Your emotions play a balanced part in your life and you use them to guide you and to tell you when things are not right. This last approach—directness—is really the only one that works consistently. You cannot run away from your more inconvenient emotions: they will not simply disappear. You may succeed in suppressing them for a time, but they will then come flooding back at inappropriate moments, so it is always best to face them, and find an outlet for them, when they first arise.

Stay Open to Your Feelings Teach yourself to move on from difficult situations without carrying too much emotional baggage.

How Relationships Develop

Research into the most common factors and qualities that contribute to the development of a relationship between two people has shown that there are fewer of them than you might think. They fall into five main groups.

These factors work to encourage the beginning of a relationship, but they also help to sustain it as it develops. If all the conditions are met, it is likely that the relationship will be successful and long-lasting. Examine a partnership or close friendship in these terms and see how many of the criteria it fulfills.

A sense of personal identity is key to a good relationship

→ **Attractiveness and accessibility** The first is an obvious feature—but however attractive someone is, they must be accessible and not beyond reach in order for a relationship to be formed.

→ **Appropriateness** For a relationship to work, each person needs to feel that the other is an equal, so that one partner does not have any huge advantage over the other.

→ **Matching needs** If only one of a couple is looking for a close relationship, while the other would be happy with a brief fling, then the union is destined to end swiftly.

→ **Partner provides interesting differences** This is a more formal way of expressing the old adage "opposites attract"—and it seems to be borne out by research.

→ **Mutual influencing** There is an expectation that each member of a couple will influence the other, and that they are responsive to one another's needs. A relationship often goes wrong when one person stops learning from the other.

TIP Even within a close relationship, make sure you behave as an individual. The partnerships that work best are formed between two independent people.

Five Steps to Emotional Confidence

To become an emotional expert, follow the five stages listed below. Think through each step and how it applies to your actions—past and present—as you go. You will find that you are examining your emotions in much greater depth than you are used to, and this may sometimes make you uncomfortable, but persist.

1 Know What You Are Feeling It is helpful to be able to name your emotions. Are you wild with rage, or merely irritated? Are you filled with love and happiness, or simply having a good time? Understand that emotions just are. Do not try to wish them away. You cannot deny yourself, or anyone else, the right to feel anything. Don't waste time thinking that an emotion is "wrong." Concentrate on what you are feeling, and develop your emotional literacy— your ability accurately to describe your emotions.

Be careful with strong feelings— treat them with respect

2 Read the Emotional Message Learn to read the messages that your emotions are sending you. If you feel hemmed in by your current relationship, for example, ask yourself why, and work out when this feeling is at its strongest, and what would make it go away. If you are upset or angry—after a difficult meeting at work, for example—try asking other people for their opinion. Help yourself to think in a more balanced way. By asking others for their thoughts about an unwelcome situation, you may discover you misread the signals and, as a result, feel mild irritation instead of seething anger.

3 Use Past Successes Generally, things pass. We cope and we move on. Rarely is a difficulty the big deal we are making it out to be. Remember a time in the past when you were depressed: you probably decided to talk to a close friend, go out for a drink, or go to a movie. And it worked. If you do the same, it's likely that it will work again. This is a coping strategy, and the more you have, the more you will be able to keep your life on an even keel. They form part of your emotional literacy toolbox.

4 Take Action Uncomfortable emotions like hurt, fear, anger, irritation, guilt, anxiety, and abandonment are there for a reason. They are telling you that things are not right and that you must take appropriate action. The sooner you take action, the more control you will have over your emotions. Sadness or hurt can be nipped in the bud before developing into depression, for example, or rage can be checked at an early stage and remain as mild irritation.

5 Focus on Positive Emotions Learn to replace negative, restricting emotions with positive alternatives that will propel you forward. Focus on what makes you feel good in life or about yourself and leave less room for bad feelings. Love, affection, enthusiasm, and commitment are all powerful emotions. Make changes in your life to allow you to experience them more frequently. Take positive steps to change both your situation and your feelings simultaneously; they influence one another.

Get to Positive

Work your way through these stages to reach positive feelings on which you can build.

Learn to recognize and acknowledge your feelings

⬇

Acquire emotional literacy— express your feelings

⬇

Use past successes to deal with the negatives

⬇

Act on what your feelings are telling you

⬇

Build on the positive

Build Dating Confidence

Dating confidence increases with practice. You need to go on dates to gain confidence, and you have to meet people in order to date, so it is up to you to go out regularly and develop your skills through experience.

Identify Your Target Market

Before embarking on the dating game, work out your target market. Think where you are most likely to meet the sort of person you have identified as your target. If you think that you would like a creative partner, for instance, visit galleries, join a film or book club, or pick an evening class in art appreciation. Take age into consideration, too, when you think about where to meet potential partners.

Put Yourself in the Right Place

You may feel safer in a group, but remember that you will also be harder to approach—think about how much more nervous you would be of walking up to a large group who you don't know, but who all know one another, than of

TECHNIQUES *to* practice

First thing in the morning on the day before an important date, use this visualization. Imagining the date as clearly as possible, all through the different stages of the evening, will help you to relax, and the more relaxed you are, the better the date will go.

• Imagine the details: chatting, walking together, eating, watching the show or movie.

• Visualize looking into your date's eyes, and them looking into yours.

• Imagine yourself as a magnet, attracting them with your gaze, your warmth, and your personality.

• Take your time envisaging all the details of your evening.

• Finish your visualization by telling yourself that this is the way the evening will go.

...alking to just one or two approachable-looking people. Going out with one or two friends is likely to

Go to the Right Places Look for people in the places where you choose to spend time. If you want to meet an art lover, for example, visit a gallery.

make it easier to meet new people, and going out by yourself is the best way of all. Remember the key points:

Get out and about

Put yourself on the relationship market

Think about the places you are most likely to find the people you want to meet

Make as many friends as possible; don't focus too strongly on finding just one special person

Market yourself well—take time and care with how you look, as well as practicing your conversation

TIP Meeting the right person for you is like winning the lottery: if you don't take part in the game, you have no chance at the winning ticket.

Building Friendships

The best route of all to finding a good relationship is to form a series of strong friendships. If your focus is primarily on finding a sexual and romantic partner, this may seem like an indirect route, but making friends is a good way to introduce yourself to a possible partner, too, and puts less pressure on a relationship at its early stages. Concentrate on being interested in a new person when you meet them—ask questions, listen, and talk; this will be more successful than practicing an impersonal pick-up routine.

Broaden Your Thinking

Spread your friendships widely—do not think in all-or-nothing terms, relying too strongly on one encounter, one evening, or even focusing too heavily on one person at

Use FORE to Make New Friends

There is a formula for getting to know someone, even if you only have five minutes with them. It is called FORE.

F FAMILY

O OCCUPATION

R RECREATION

E EDUCATION

It works on the principle that these are the conversational areas in which, if you ask questions, you will get to know someone new most quickly. You do not need pick-up lines—in fact, they can deflect you from getting to know someone. What you are doing is finding out if you have common interests, views about life, background, and aspirations. You can then progress further to discover more, or move on to another person you find interesting, leaving your new acquaintance with a positive impression of you.

CASE study: Overcoming Shyness

Jane was very shy and found making friends difficult. She would turn down invitations to social gatherings rather than risk approaching strangers. She was so fearful of being "stuck for words" that she ended up with nothing to say, and her social horizons were severely restricted by her shyness. She was invited to attend a wedding reception at which she would know very few people. After reading about the FORE Formula, she accepted, practicing the principles on her way to the party. Once there, after initial awkwardness, she found she was able to approach other guests and strike up conversations successfully, keeping the formula in mind.

- *The formula worked because it took the focus off Jane, allowing her to engage in conversation with genuine interest—losing the air of a "shy" person, she became more approachable herself.*
- *The `rules of the formula made it easy to follow, reviving flagging conversation and leaving space for someone else to speak if she ran out of things to say.*

first. Practice your social encounters at moments when you feel relaxed, experimenting with different types of people and different conversational approaches and seeing which kind of technique works best for you.

Create a Good Impression

Aim to look good, the best you can, whether that means getting a good haircut, buying a new shirt, or wearing your favorite outfit. All the dating makeover programs shown on television spend considerable time on how their subjects look, because they know it works, both in terms of building someone's confidence, and therefore causing them to project in an attractive way, and in improving how they appear to others.

TIP Remember that looking good shows respect for yourself, as well as a regard for other people.

Making New Friends

Supportive friendships and relationships are good for you. Research has shown that people are more likely to feel well, and less likely to have mental and physical problems, if they are in loving relationships.

Widen Your Interests

New friendships mean new interests—in people, cultures, opinions, experiences, or hobbies. You might meet someone who suggests you join their evening class or book club; they might invite you on an activity vacation, or encourage you to pursue a

New interests can be a springboard for greater confidence

shared interest you have not, so far, had the courage, energy, or company to explore. Your address book will become fuller as you meet friends of friends, while adding another focus to your leisure time. As your social circle widens, so will your social and emotional confidence. You will have a wider network of emotional support and feel confident in new areas of your life.

Nurture Your Friendships

It is important to remember, however, that friendships, whether new or established, long-distance or close (in terms of proximity), need nurturing. Technology helps with this enormously. If phone calls, cards, or letters prove too demanding, you should be able to find time for a quick email or text message to friends you are unable to see for weeks or even months. Friendship does not depend on face-to-face interaction, and you will have friends with whom you can pick up easily after long absences, but

TIP When you talk to new people, try to sound upbeat, positive, and interested; ask yourself if you would want to be your friend.

friendship can fade, if not wither, without some nourishment. Friendships are two-way streets, and you should be prepared to support as well as be supported. Unlike romantic relationships, friendships are generally not exclusive, leaving greater room for ambiguity and a need for confirmation.

Get Positive Feedback

Good friends can boost your self-esteem. If you feel your self-confidence undermined and in need of some positive feedback and reinforcement before a challenging interview or occasion, ask your friends to tell you what they see as your best qualities, abilities, and achievements. Ask them to name the top three things about you that they like. Ask them how they would describe you to a new person, or try imagining what they would say. Next time you need a confidence boost, repeat their words to yourself.

Audit Your Relationships

You will have a network of different types of relationships in your life, whether platonic or romantic. Some will be more supportive, some more demanding than others. In some you will be the parent (either literally or figuratively), in others the child. Conduct a relationship audit and work out who has a positive or negative effect on your confidence. Do this in your head or on paper. Put a plus or minus sign against each entry to make their influence clearer in your mind. The chart could feature all your romantic and non-romantic relationships, including partners, parents, children, peers, siblings, friends, and colleagues—or be restricted to certain elements, in this case your friends.

A Typical Audit Consider how each person interacts with you on an emotional or practical level.

My Friendship with Andrei—Relationship Audit

- Does he make me feel better about myself when we are together, and afterward?
- Does he undermine my self-confidence?
- Can I really confide in him?
- Can I completely trust him?
- How would he respond if I had an emotional crisis?
- What would he do if I really needed his practical help?
- Am I the child or the parent in our relationship?
- Is our relationship mutually supportive?
- Do we treat each other as equals?
- Does he try to control me? Do I try to control him?
- Does he support me in my career/personal decisions?
- Does he offer me constructive criticism?

Assessing a Friendship

Spend more time with positive friends and less time with negative people. You can tell which is which by asking yourself which set of statements is true.

I feel confident and positive when I am with friend A	I feel low self-esteem when I am with friend B
I feel good about myself after I have seen friend A	I always feel bad about myself after I have seen friend B
I should spend more time with friend A	I should spend less time with friend B

Listen to the Answers

The answers, together with other questions they may trigger, will help you assess whether you should spend more or less time with particular individuals. Some people like to have friends with less confidence—it helps them feel better about themselves and allows them, also, to feel superior and in control. They act as the parent in a friendship. Consider if this is true of any of your own relationships. Think how you interact with your friends and if you consciously try to boost their self-esteem.

Use Your Audit Constructively

You may find when conducting the friendship audit that you identify a particular person whom you trust completely, someone who always offers constructive criticism alongside encouragement and support—a confidence supplier, not a sapper. You may even start to think of them in a different light—as a potential partner. Friendships, like romantic relationships, need maintenance, and will have good and bad moments, and their share of compromise, commitment, and responsibility-taking.

TIP **Keep an open mind about all your relationships; don't keep them in labeled compartments.**

Relationship Confidence

Relationships are wonderful, but they are also fragile. Anything built on an emotional foundation will have its weaknesses and stress points. You and your partner need to keep the foundations as strong as possible, and maintain the relationship like a building, giving it additional support and perhaps a spring cleaning or a new coat of paint from time to time. Having found a partner with whom you feel confident, you need to work on remaining confident within that relationship.

Travel Light

Try to travel light into a relationship. Arriving laden with emotional baggage will make moving forward much slower, and may simply trip you up as you go. Leave any preconceptions, about yourself or relationships in general, behind. If you were badly hurt in your last relationship, don't wait for it happen again, or you may prompt it to happen. As you move into a relationship, think of it as moving into a new house, and bring with you only the things you really need for a positive environment.

Keep a Positive Image of Yourself

View your relationship as a coming together of two equals, through mutual, positive, active choice. Remember your own worth, your contribution, your competence, your appeal. Don't try to be the perfect partner: the pursuit of perfection undermines self-esteem. It is unrealistic and leads to dissatisfaction. Settle for "perfectly good." Aim for perspective, not perfection—this applies to your view of yourself and your relationship, but it is a successful formula to use in much wider areas of your life, including your career, outside interests, and contribution to society.

TIP **Think of your confidence as an emotional trampoline. It gives you the energy and resilience to bounce back from pitfalls in your relationship.**

Rescue Your Relationship

When you and your partner hit a stumbling block in your relationship, bear in mind that your confidence may well be vulnerable and exposed, and could become a casualty.

Having a coping strategy at your disposal can help protect you and your relationship, before either partner feels too vulnerable.

→ Acknowledge and identify the problem.
→ Resist any temptation to assume all the blame in your own mind.
→ Write down your concerns, your needs, your involvement in the issue, and a possible way forward.
→ Agree when would be a good time to discuss the issue.
→ Outline the issues clearly in turn, allowing each other time and space to explain, without interruption and without losing your temper.
→ Discuss the next step; agree on a compromise, a solution, or an action plan.

Assess Your Relationship Don't ever take your partner or your relationship for granted. Talk often, and be open and truthful about how you feel.

Summary: Confidence with Others

Confidence affects all aspects of relationships, from forming friendships to developing a partnership and, once you have it, will give you the resilience to bounce back from setbacks. Learn from this summary how confidence interconnects four key areas of relationship building.

How Confidence Builds Relationships

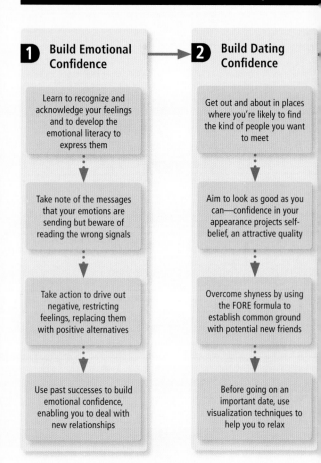

1 **Build Emotional Confidence**

Learn to recognize and acknowledge your feelings and to develop the emotional literacy to express them

↓

Take note of the messages that your emotions are sending but beware of reading the wrong signals

↓

Take action to drive out negative, restricting feelings, replacing them with positive alternatives

↓

Use past successes to build emotional confidence, enabling you to deal with new relationships

2 **Build Dating Confidence**

Get out and about in places where you're likely to find the kind of people you want to meet

↓

Aim to look as good as you can—confidence in your appearance projects self-belief, an attractive quality

↓

Overcome shyness by using the FORE formula to establish common ground with potential new friends

↓

Before going on an important date, use visualization techniques to help you to relax

3 Build Friendships that Last

Focus on building strong friendships and spread your net wide—you might well find a partner this way

See your social and emotional confidence building as your social circle widens and you develop new interests

Nurture your friendships with care—they require nourishing on both sides to grow healthy and strong

Audit your relationships, then boost your confidence by spending more time with positive people

4 Build Confidence in Relationships

As you move into a relationship, think of it as moving house—cast aside emotional baggage that might undermine it

Don't try to be a "perfect" partner, which undermines self-esteem— and don't expect perfection from your partner

Rejuvenate flagging relationships by giving them periodic "health checks"

Think of confidence as an emotional trampoline that empowers you to bounce back from pitfalls

Keep the Relationship Alive

If your confidence in your relationship has plummeted, take a careful look at the way in which you and your partner are relating to one another. Tired relationships can be rejuvenated if you spot the signs in time.

Health-Check Your Relationship

Relationships don't need to have reached crisis point to have problems. Ask yourself the following questions to conduct a health check on your partnership:

Our Relationship Now

- Do we go out less now than we used to, and enjoy fewer celebrations (birthdays, special days, anniversaries) than we did?
- Do we have a tendency to put each other down in front of our friends?
- Have we started to eat meals in front of the television instead of sitting at the table and enjoying the opportunity for conversation?
- Do we both take a stronger interest than we used to in other members of the opposite sex when we are out together?
- Do we read in bed instead of making love?
- Do we feel that we are both stuck in a rut?

If the answer to the majority of these questions is "yes," then your relationship needs a closer look. While it's normal to settle down a little after the first flush of romantic interest, this doesn't mean that it's natural that you should start taking one another for granted. Give your relationship a shot in the arm by paying it extra attention for a week or two.

Reinvigorating the Relationship

Try taking the following steps over a period of two to three weeks to test the underlying health of your partnership. They will reveal whether all is fundamentally well with your relationship—or not.

→ Only say positive things to and about your partner for a week.
→ Think about the qualities and attributes that first brought you together. Focus on them and compliment them.
→ Make some dates in your planner to go out alone together a couple of times a week.
→ Take up a common interest together—something you've always wanted to try, but never got around to.

At the end of the week, review how you both feel. Has your relationship improved? If not, ask yourselves why not. Are neither of you really prepared to put in the effort? If there are signs of life, do you want to continue with the makeover? If so, examine which activities worked best, and give yourselves more of them.

Analyze What Is Wrong

If the makeover seems to have little positive effect on your relationship you will need to consider, and discuss, the next step. Keep talking about it as much and for as long as you can. Don't terminate your relationship too easily—regrets over unconsidered endings like this can damage you in the long term. Don't let the process undermine your confidence to the point where you give up through lack of energy or the future of your partnership, either.

TIP Whether you decide to stay with your relationship or to end it, make sure that sustaining it or ending it are positive experiences—it is possible.

Make the Decision

If, sadly, one or both of you decide that the relationship is dead, then you must have some difficult conversations. Try to keep talking—a relationship that ends in silence will be more damaging to your confidence than one in which you maintained communication and mutual respect. Remember that there is life beyond the relationship, and that there are a number of strategies that will help you get over the failure of this one and to prepare for the next.

Strategies for Coping

Grieve for the loss of your partner. Do not pretend that you do not care when you did, and you still do. Even though there are steps you can take to get over the grieving process and to help you move on, you should still think in terms of months rather than weeks if your relationship was a long one. Don't expect an unrealistically fast rate of recovery.

5 minute FIX

Spend five minutes each day focusing on your future. Be compassionate toward yourself and say:

- I am confident, competent, and attractive.
- Now I am a more experienced person.
- I am taking only positive things forward into the future.

Use Visualization

Visualize your ex-partner at their worst—perhaps in the middle of a fight. This will enable you mentally to withdraw affection: the reverse process of when you first met and fell in love. Remember when you used to imagine all their endearing habits and gestures; now you are simply turning that process on its head to help you regain your emotional control and to move on with your life. Throw out reminders of your partner—gather up photographs, cards, or presents you do not want to keep, cut them up, and throw them out. This is a symbolic act of termination and spiritual cleansing.

TECHNIQUES *to practice*

Don't listen to your inner critic when a relationship comes to an end.
Take ten minutes out to do a relationship audit of a different kind:

1 Think what positive, and new, things you have discovered about yourself.

2 Assess the ways in which you developed emotionally within the relationship. You may see that you are stronger than you realized, and you may come to appreciate the positive things that it brought you.

3 Consider how you can apply your new skills to other relationships

4 Focus on the legacy of the relationship, not the responsibility for its end.

Free Yourself for the Future

Removing reminders is both a cathartic and a preventive measure—removing the premature temptation to rake over the past, by going through letters or other keepsakes from your ex-partner with nostalgia and regret. It is important to look forward to the future—rather than back to the past—with anticipation and hope for new possibilities and horizons. Remind yourself from time to time just why you split up with your ex-partner and feel confident in that decision. Don't idealize a relationship that's over, but respect the past relationship—going into lengthy analyses of why it was bad will not help you to look forward. Don't launch into a new relationship too soon, but try out different ways to meet people. Go away for a weekend or a short break. Be proactive in your forward thinking, not passive in your retrospection.

TIP Lay your past relationship calmly to rest, and look forward happily. A postmortem won't bring you a resurrection.

Take Stock

Make new friends and date if you want to, but allow yourself one month for every year your relationship lasted before you think about falling in love again. Do not expect to feel love for a while; trying to force your emotions will lead you to make mistakes. In the meantime, be discriminating—don't determine to go out regardless of who asks you, and choose potential dates with care. Take time to choose, rather than gratefully taking the first person who shows an interest in you. Tell yourself that you are between partners at the moment, and if you find yourself thinking, "I will never have a relationship with anyone as great as my last partner again," particularly if you were not the one who chose to end the relationship, banish the thought.

Keep a Journal

It can help to jot down how you feel in the days and weeks after you split up with someone. Journals offer you the opportunity to look back and see how well you are doing over a period, even though it may not feel like it on a bad day. Getting your thoughts and feelings down on paper helps in a number of ways.

→ You can release any residual anger and hurt, you can detach from your feelings to a degree, and you can learn more about yourself.

→ Read the entries again later and see just how much what you think is affected by how you feel. It does not have to take too much time.

→ A few minutes each day is all that is needed. Do it at night when you are relaxed, or at times when you feel really angry or upset. You choose the time to write, the amount you put down, and the form it takes.

Relish Your Single Status Just as being part of a couple has its advantages, so does being single. Take the time to see friends, explore new activities, and spend time enjoying your own company. Build your relationship—with yourself.

Enjoy Being Single

Spend time with your positive, supportive friends. They will provide the encouragement and extra resilience you may find you need when your confidence takes a dip. Try to go out even when you do not really feel like it. Accept one in every two invitations that sound appealing, even if you find that you can't accept them all. Avoid the temptation to curl up in front of the television with a box of tissues. Go out with your single friends and see how interesting and fulfilling their lives are. See life from a different angle and gain a new perspective. Enjoy new and different experiences and influences. Make a wish list and try to check off at least two items on it every week.

TIP **See your single status as an opportunity, not a sentence. Enjoy being selfish for once.**

Confidence
at Work

4

Confidence in the workplace is a key issue in many people's lives. You may need to negotiate a job move, either within your organization or into a new one, ask for promotion or fresh challenges, or decide to set up your own business. People do settle for second-, or even third-, best at work; this chapter challenges that compromise and shows you how to:

- Become more visible at work
- Discover your strengths and weaknesses
- Learn the skill of mind mapping
- Develop successful interview techniques
- Present with panache
- Consider setting up your own business

Becoming Visible at Work

Some people are content to work conscientiously but invisibly for years. The very fact that you are reading this probably means you are aware of that and don't want it to happen to you—you want to make an impact.

Be Seen and Heard

The management guru Charles Handy told a revealing anecdote of how he was asked by his wife in his early days of employment if he was proud of his work. His reply, that it was all right as work went, met with the riposte that she did not want to spend the rest of her life with someone prepared to settle for "all right." Making yourself visible and raising your head above the professional parapet is not without risk. But taking a risk—and it doesn't have to be a big one—is part of the process of beginning to be heard in the workplace. It's like being abroad and speaking to someone in a foreign language for the first time—you risk making mistakes, but, unless you brave it, there will be no discussion and you will not learn anything.

> **Self-belief is as important as anyone else's belief in you**

Choose Confidence

Like any relationship, that between company and staff is a two-way street. Just as confident families play a key role in nurturing and supporting confident children, so confident companies will help reinforce the self-esteem of their staff, and vice versa. Confidence, like positive energy, is infectious. It filters down, sideways, and back up again, from the boardroom to the mailroom and along into management. If you feel that your workplace is sapping your energy and confidence, then you need to consider changing your professional environment from the inside, exploring your options for working elsewhere, or changing your response to work and your workplace.

Make Yourself Visible

There are several ways to change your professional visibility from barely there to high-impact. The following suggestions are all positive ways to get noticed.

They are just some suggestions, however. They may help to trigger your own ideas about how to make a difference in your particular role, or specific to the company in which you work.

→ Volunteer to take on the tasks or projects that others avoid or dislike—and deliver on them.

→ Offer your own ideas for new solutions to existing problems.

→ Consistently deliver to deadline or ahead of it.

→ Ask for greater challenges at your work review.

→ Be prepared to present and justify your results.

→ Identify areas of poor performance and suggest a strategy to remedy them.

→ Be proactive, not reactive. Stand out from the crowd.

→ Be positive about change, not defensive.

Speak Up Voicing your opinions may be daunting at first. But your colleagues will appreciate your input, and you will soon learn to speak up confidently.

Know Your Strengths

As part of your strategy, write a list of your strengths in the workplace. Consider what particular cluster of skills you bring to your job or organization, and how they are used. If you find it difficult to relate your strengths to work, try thinking of the contribution you make to the lives of the important people in your personal life—family, friends, and colleagues. Consider how they impact on your life and use those ideas as prompters in your own self-assessment.

Good qualities in personal life can always be applied at work

Ask Your Secret Service Group

Ask the close friends and colleagues who make up your Secret Service Group what they consider to be your greatest strengths. They are on the receiving end of your influence upon their lives, and ideally placed to assess your contribution and value. Getting their objective, honest feedback about your positive attributes will give you the extra confidence to recognize your talents and add them to your list. Don't underestimate your input—either at work or in your personal life. To help you get started on your list, try asking yourself some of the following questions about your interaction with friends and family:

- What positive influence do you have on them?
- How do you impact on their well-being?
- Do you provide practical advice or help?
- Are you a good listener? Can you keep a secret?
- Do you offer support and encouragement?
- Are you an honest, straightforward, positive, solid, and reliable friend?

TIP Be confident in your career choice and capitalize on your strengths to progress it.

Take the best of your qualities and mentally roll them together into a group of skills that will reinforce your career.

Be Aware of Weaknesses

Now write down your weaknesses in the workplace. Again, ask your Secret Service Group for honest feedback about these. Acknowledging them does not show weakness, but will add to your strengths. Self-knowledge and self-awareness are keys to professional or personal success. You have to know your limits in all areas of life. You can work on your weaknesses at work with extra skills training.

Value Your Strengths

Having identified your strengths, the next step is to build on them. Don't assume that everyone else is just as good as you. Your strengths are your unique selling point, so learn to capitalize on them, and to send the message clearly to others. If you are good at research but poor at selling, acknowledge that and focus on what you excel at. Don't expect to be good at everything. Excelling in a particular area is something to celebrate.

Dismiss Your Fears

Choose your worst fear or embarrassment. Mentally, put it in the blank space left for it, below, then work your way through the stages

→ What if................ happened? What would be the consequence?
→ How foolish would I look? And in front of whom?
→ How would I cope with being made to look ridiculous?
→ Could I use humor or irony to enlist people's sympathy?
→ What would be the final consequence of my fear coming to pass?

This listing of the consequences of bad things happening—a version of the exercise in Chapter 2—will bring you to the point at which you are able to say "so what?" and get on with your life.

Learn to Mind-Map

In 1974, Tony Buzan launched the concept of Mind Maps®. His ideas have since become popular worldwide. They work on the principle that words can trigger the brain into radiating an entire network of associations.

Understand the Concept

Mind mapping, or concept mapping, involves writing down a central idea and then thinking of new and related ideas that radiate out from the center. The map reflects the way you think, making connections from a central point without an imposed structure. The two-dimensional format replaces the traditional concept of list-making and stimulates nonlinear thinking and problem-solving. It allows you to roam the huge landscape of your brain.

Mind maps offer a picture of the thinking process

Use the Concept

Mind mapping helps you to store, organize, summarize, and consolidate information, and think through complex problems. With a mind map, you can present information in a way that shows the overall structure of your subject. It is a great aid for brainstorming. Having written down your central theme, you can then add anything that comes into your head, based around this central core concept. It makes memorizing and retrieving facts easier, helping you to exploit the enormous computer-cum-library operating inside your head. The simple mind map opposite demonstrates the concept, but you need to practice and develop your own style to derive maximum effect from this powerful tool. You will learn how to use it to structure reports, plan presentations, and, importantly, to prepare for interviews.

All words are pegs to hang ideas on.

American proverb

Make a Mind Map

Try to make a map of your life as it is now. Think freely while you are constructing your map—the idea is to go with the stream of your consciousness, not to analyze.

→ Think of an area of your life that seems unresolved, and that you feel needs some creative work. Start with a key word, written in capitals, or an image, in the center of a blank page (turn it sideways for extra space). This is your central idea (it might be "promotion", "contentment" or "relationships"— keep it broad. Use colors for extra vibrancy and energy. Colors and images stimulate the memory.

→ Only use one word, or two at most, per line.

→ Connect your main, curved branches to the central image and connect your second and third level, similarly curved, branches to the first and second levels, and so on.

→ Your mind should be left as free as possible during this process. Analysis and order can come later.

Free Thinking The loose associations encouraged by mind mapping will help you to make creative links that you might not have thought of otherwise.

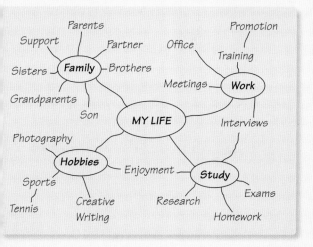

Use Mind Maps at Work

Mind maps can help you within a professional context, saving time and increasing efficiency. You can put all your questions and answers on just one page instead of making separate, confusing lists. The process allows for extra flexibility in a way that linear note-taking does not. You can see the whole picture and all the details at the same time, allowing you to do "big picture thinking" with all the "small picture," detailed information fixed in your mind. A mind map taps into the way our brains actually work, helping us to be more creative and to retain more data.

Make Maps Work for You

Try mind-mapping a problem at work, then show it to a colleague so that you can brainstorm solutions together. Mind-map a relationship with a client, and, as that relationship develops, add new branches, updating your map with new developments. If you need to get perspective on a difficult working relationship, mind maps are also an effective tool. They help you to see both the issues and fresh creative pathways to the solution.

CASE study: Clarifying the Problem

Chang, a human resources manager, felt overworked, but her options were restricted by family obligations. She discussed this at a problem-solving workshop. The group did a mind map of all Chang's issues. They learned that, since the departure of a colleague, she was doing two jobs, and that she had not discussed the situation with her boss, feeling that he should have discussed it with her.

Similarly, she had not discussed her frustration with her husband.

• *The mind map made it clear that Chang's lack of assertiveness lay at the root of her issues.*
• *Chang realized she had to make her feelings clear: she could see the results of her past actions.*
• *Discussions with her husband and her boss led to professional and domestic improvements.*

Work on Mind Maps Together

Mind mapping can work as a powerful tool for a group to problem-solve or to think creatively, as well as for the individual. Try a mind-mapping session to encourage your team to work together to find creative solutions.

Thinking Styles Mind mapping teaches the members of a team more about how they think—both independently, and as part of a group.

Involve Everyone Mind mapping is an activity in which everyone can join, regardless of status or office hierarchy.

Use a Visualizer Appoint one person to write the mind map out as it develops. This ensures that the session doesn't get too chaotic.

TIP Use mind mapping in a group both to arrive at a clear picture of a problem or concern, and to gain a clearer picture of how your colleagues' minds work.

Preparing for Interviews

Interview confidence comes with planning, preparation, and practice. You need to behave in a proactive way, both beforehand and in the interview itself. This section looks at good planning and preparation techniques.

Learn about the Interview Process

At some stage in your professional career, if you wish to move on within an organization or join another, you will have to become confident at interviews. An interview may not be an ideal context in which to get to know and make decisions about people, but it is the way in which most organizations operate. It is important to remember that many professionals are not skilled at the interview process, some talk rather than question, others look for like-minded individuals rather than risk introducing people with different viewpoints, backgrounds, or visions.

Boardroom profiles

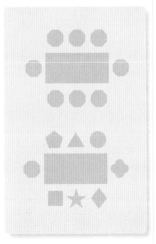

Strength in Diversity The group at the top employs people with similar mind-sets and skills; the one below has a number of differently skilled people. Which do you think will be stronger?

Look for Diversity

Some of the top companies actively recruit staff with diverse talents and backgrounds. They are aware of the need to mirror their own customer base, demographic, and needs with diversity in their own organizations. They embrace new ideas and different skills, and operate a policy of inclusion. They are aware that multi-skilled teams are highly effective when handling clients with a range of specific demands. The combination of talent, new perspective,

Effective Applications

HIGH IMPACT

- Researching the best company in your chosen field
- Investigating company policy on points that are important to you
- Attending open days to get a feel for the company
- Checking out competitors in the field with potential for takeover
- Talking to people with direct experience of the company to which you are applying

NEGATIVE IMPACT

- Wasting time applying to unsuitable companies
- Finding out too late that policy is not in line with your views
- Being handicapped at interview through lack of research
- Failing to realize the company is in line for purchase
- Finding out only after joining the company that it has a poor employment record

and wide experience makes for a very powerful team. If the board is made up of people who see things through the same eyes, and who share most of the same skills, no new vision will be brought to the mix, and the company will run the risk of becoming complacent in its approach.

Choose the Right Company

Start your hunt for the right company for you with some research into the best companies operating in your field of choice. Many business periodicals compile an annual list of the best companies to work for, and a look at these could be a good starting point. Do more in-depth research on the Internet and read relevant market journals. Approach this task with focus and determination. Any old job in any old company is not the strategy. It can result in your being as unhappy in a new environment as you were in your old one. Try not to fall into the "take it now" trap, resulting in your leaping at the first offer instead of waiting for the right job.

TIP The strongest companies are made up of like-minded people with diverse skill sets

Learn about Psychometric Tests

Today, more and more organizations use psychometric tests. They are a way of assessing a candidate's personality profile or skills in a structured way, and help the interviewer to assess if you have the right mix of abilities, personal qualities, and interest—that is, to establish if you fit the job. For employers, they are useful for sifting out large numbers of applicants at an early stage in the process, thereby saving them time and money. For you, they are a good way of making sure the job fits you.

Have Confidence in the Tests

The more interviews you attend, the more comfortable you will become with the psychometric process. Some employers will make sample test questions available ahead of the interview; if they do, take advantage of it, so that you will feel more relaxed when it comes to the real thing.

Learn How the Tests Work

The word "psychometric" literally means "measuring the brain." Do not let this intimidate you; the tests are devised to measure certain characteristics and undergo rigorous trials. A good organization will use qualified assessors and give you feedback.

→ They may be administered on paper or computer, and you may be asked to take them in a test center or online.

→ They are widely used by companies operating in many areas, including IT, engineering, energy, banking, consulting, accountancy, and retail, with specific tests aimed at identifying the best candidates for specific jobs.

→ There are no right or wrong answers, and the interviewers use the reports not as absolute truths, but as a means to explore your character and strengths.

Research in Advance

Before going to an interview, find out if you will be taking a psychometric test. These points will help you in your preparation and your performance:

- Remember, employers are looking for different personalities to match different positions within their company, so the best policy is honesty.
- The tests are set up to detect if you are lying or being unrealistic about your abilities, so don't invent or exaggerate your skills.
- Be consistent in your responses—don't try to please.
- Ask for a copy of the results. It is your right to be able to comment on the written report.
- Remember, your answers offer insights into your character—not absolute truths.

Ask what the weighting of the report is during the interview, and how key a role in the choice of candidate it plays. A good company should reply that it helps them to ask the right questions at interview. Greater importance than that indicates a misuse of the test. If you feel they have misused the test, remember its name so you can report the company to the test supplier.

Taking Psychometric Tests

HIGH IMPACT	NEGATIVE IMPACT
• Answering clearly and straightforwardly	• Prevaricating or exaggerating in your answers
• Approaching the test positively—it's for your benefit	• Looking on the test with suspicion and distrust
• Asking interested questions about the test at interview	• Offering different answers at interview from those in your test

Gain Interview Confidence

If even the word "interview" makes you feel anxious, this section offers techniques to help. Visualize yourself replying to the question, "Why should we hire you?" with a confident, "Because you can't afford not to."

Prepare to Impress

Preparation is key to performing well at interviews. Looking like a startled rabbit in the headlights of a car when the person across the desk asks you what you can bring to his or her company is not going to help you impress or progress. You need to have answers ready to probable, predictable, and inevitable questions, with fluency and confidence attached. Just as in any other situation in life, you will feel much more assured, and come over as such, if you know what to expect and how to react and respond impressively. Remember, you have to make an impression, look better than the rest, and offer something unique—or another applicant will get the job. Congratulate yourself on getting to the interview stage and start preparing.

Good Interview Technique

HIGH IMPACT

- Taking directions to the building with you, and arriving on time, or a few minutes early
- Dressing neatly and appropriately, with good grooming and accessories
- Coming armed with a copy of your résumé, a pen, and notes with your questions and company research
- Looking, listening, and behaving as if you really want the job

NEGATIVE IMPACT

- Keeping the interviewer waiting; saying you found the building hard to find
- Looking unkempt, in an unimaginative outfit without any individual touches
- Forgetting to bring your résumé, notes, or research; asking the interviewer for a pen and paper to write with
- Appearing nervous, negative, and lacking in confidence

Mind Map an Interview

Mind mapping an interview as part of your preparation is both speedy and helpful. You can put all your questions, answers, and notes on a single, landscape-format page.

Fix them in your mind as a mirror of how you are thinking. Put "Job Interview" at the center as the core message, and consider using some of the following as your branches, but remember, it is your mind map and you may wish to add different ones:

→ Dress and grooming
→ Timing
→ Body language
→ Preparation: questions and answers
→ Experience and qualifications

→ Achievements, personal and professional
→ People skills, with examples
→ Goals and ambitions
→ Strengths and weaknesses
→ Post-interview follow-up

Research the Interview

Try to find out the format of the interview in advance—if it will be conducted by a panel or on a one-to-one basis, if group activity will be involved or if you will be asked to make a presentation, and if so to whom/how many and for how long. Discover if any tests, psychometric or other, will form part of the procedure. Ask if you can look around the offices afterward and talk to some of the staff (use your judgment; this may prove to be a more appropriate question on a second interview). The more you know ahead of the interview, the more prepared you will appear.

Watch, listen, and learn. You can't know it all yourself; anyone who thinks they do is destined for mediocrity.

Donald Trump

Present Yourself Positively

Think facts and focus when presenting your achievements to a prospective new employer. They will want to know what combination of experience and skills you can offer, and what positive impact you will make on their team.

They will need positive evidence that you are a work in progress, with further potential. They will be looking for a leading-edge candidate. Think through these points:

Prepare Your Answers

- Why your qualifications and experience relate to the job
- How you increased business, profitability, or turnover for your company (with percentages)
- How, and to what degree, you expanded its customer base (with percentages)
- How you managed a large or difficult team, motivated unwilling staff, or developed staff roles
- How you handled personality clashes
- How you recruited effective staff or motivated/ removed inefficient employees
- How you improved quality control or deadlines
- What innovative products or ideas you introduced
- How you avoided crises or solved them
- What projects you put in place/completed/rescued
- How you stay up to date in your field

TIP Learn your own market value and worth by asking head-hunters or contacts. Use it later as a negotiating tool if necessary.

Prepare Your Answers

Think of the questions that you will certainly be asked. Prepare up to four positive answers to each possible question. Your mind map will help you remember them. For example, if you are asked how your boss would describe you, you might say, positive, creative, hard-working, efficient, a problem solver, and calm in a crisis. Don't include weaknesses at this stage. Wait to be asked about those. Make sure you have questions prepared. Having researched the company thoroughly, ask relevant questions that allow you to demonstrate your knowledge.

5 minute FIX

Use these pages as your condensed preparation and survival manual.

- The few minutes before an interview are often the most nerve-racking.

- Photocopy these pages and take them with you as a last-minute aid, to read as you wait in the lobby.

Be Clear and Honest

Illustrate your answers with examples, giving succinct evidence of your skills. You will lose impact if your accounts of problem-solving or firefighting are too discursive. Explain the problem, your solution, and the successful outcome, briefly and without digressions. If asked to talk someone through your résumé, select relevant highlights. Leave the humdrum details as they stand, but explain any skeletons, gaps, or sudden departures as constructively, but honestly, as you can. When asked why you are looking to move, do not talk in negative terms about your present employer. Focus on your goals, and your desire for more responsibility, or fresh challenges or markets. Be prepared to answer questions about what you see as your weaknesses. Knowing what you are less good at shows self-awareness. Try to make strengths of your weaknesses if possible. "I have been told I am a perfectionist" is an extreme example. Explain how you confront and rectify your weak areas.

Perform at Your Best

Before you enter the room, try to relax. You can be relaxed, positive, and dynamic at the same time; this does not mean laid-back (which can manifest as a "don't-care" attitude), but calm and confident. Try to get your body language and mind set to convey the same message. "You are looking for a solution and I am it. You want me and I want to work for you." Maintain this throughout the interview. After the interview, send a note thanking the interviewer for their time and confirming your interest in the job. If you are rejected, look on it as a learning experience. Ask for feedback about your performance, and for constructive criticism to help you in the future. Remain positive and keep applying for the jobs that appeal to you.

TECHNIQUES
to practice

To calm pre-interview nerves, visualize that you have been offered the job already. Enact the following positive scenario in your mind to reinforce it:

1 You are already seated at your new desk. All you have to do is get over this small hurdle of an interview and you can start work in your new role.

2 Visualize the interview, your confident entry into the room, a pleasant round of introductions, and your calm appraisal of the interviewer or panel in front of you.

3 Imagine your first well-received answer, followed by a lively discourse, with an interesting exchange of views.

4 Imagine yourself enjoying the process, receiving encouraging feedback, and leaving the room with a positive feeling and a confident handshake.

TIP Visualize success to help it happen. Your brain is programmed by what you see and hear, but also by the breadth of your imagination.

Project Your Enthusiasm

Looking smart in an interview is important, but looking enthusiastic is just as vital. This is not a natural situation, and you may need to remind yourself to project the right body language. Use controlled gestures, smile, and tilt your head to one side. The first few minutes will be spent establishing rapport, so listen actively as the interviewer gives you information about the job and the company.

Make Eye Contact
Look the interviewer confidently in the eye.

Lean Forward Express your interest by leaning toward the interviewer as you talk.

Clasp Your Hands
Loosely clasped hands help you to seem open, accessible, and relaxed.

Summary: Confident Interviews

You've applied for the job and been shortlisted for an interview. Now you need to think ahead and be proactive before and during the interview. Use this summary as your pathway to a confident interview, giving yourself the best opportunity to achieve your goal.

Work Your Way to Confidence

1 Plan and Research

Mind-map your interview so that you can focus your thoughts on the key elements involved

Analyze your strengths and weaknesses in relation to the job description—don't expect a perfect fit

Check the format of the interview so that you can prepare for any aptitude or psychometric tests

Find out more about the company—talk to people who have dealt with them and check out competitors

2 Questions and Answers

Make a list of probable, predictable, and inevitable questions and prepare up to four answers for each

Keep your answers positive; focus on the experience and skills you can offer, with examples of your achievements

Prepare upbeat answers to your perceived weaknesses and be ready to explain gaps in your resume and sudden departures

Prepare questions that display your knowledge of the company and ask about the weighting given to any tests

3 On the Day

Dress neatly and appropriately, with good grooming and accessories

Arrive at the interview on time or a few minutes early, armed with résumé, pen, notes, and company research

Try to relax before you enter the room—visualizing a successful outcome helps to calm the nerves

Enter the room calm and confident, knowing that you have prepared thoroughly

4 In the Interview

Project enthusiasm through your body language—look, listen, and behave as if you really want the job

Give honest and direct answers—think fact and focus when illustrating your achievements

Focus on positive reasons for changing jobs—don't talk negatively about your present employer

After the interview, send a note of thanks, confirming your interest in the job

Make Meetings Work

Efficient meetings are attended by relevant staff, follow a crafted agenda and a strict time limit, and are led by an assertive chairperson. Learn to become a more confident meeting participant, whatever your role.

Be a Strong Chairperson

How many dull meetings have you attended? Once in the chair, try some of these innovative approaches to inject interest, stimulate contributions, and establish your assertiveness. Choose alternative venues. Try shortening meetings to create greater urgency. Introduce prizes for the best contribution. Try brainstorming, but restrict it to a specific time frame. Encourage those present to try out and take responsibility for their ideas. Invite someone to chair half the meeting in your place.

Be a Confident Participant

If meetings sap your confidence and make you self-conscious about voicing your own opinion, work through this meeting strategy. It should help boost your confidence in your contribution

→ Make sure you read the agenda in advance and research any issues about which you are uncertain.

→ Rehearse responses to important, personally relevant items.

→ Arrive early to compose yourself and find a good seat.

→ Do not waste time or sap confidence comparing yourself to others, who may appear more confident or knowledgeable.

→ Stand out, don't blend in—contributions bring notice and success. Having a good idea after the meeting is too late.

→ Don't let your inner voice undermine your opinion. Let your own voice underline it.

→ Leave the meeting knowing what you have to do next.

Ensure Efficient Meetings

First, check that the meeting is really necessary. Choose the best day and time. Friday at 5 p.m. isn't a good choice for a brainstorming meeting, for example—people will already be thinking about getting home for their weekend—but it might be ideal for a short get-together to deal with a specific problem. Set clear objectives, invite only relevant participants, and prepare an agenda with stated goals, together with key steps to achieving those goals by its close. Distribute the agenda in advance and make sure they are briefed to discuss itemized topics. If the meeting has been scheduled far in advance, it is worth sending an email confirming it to all the attendees the day before.

Run Meetings with Confidence

Start the meeting promptly, stating a clear time frame at the outset. Follow the agenda strictly. Your role is as effective facilitator, keeping participants focused and resolving potential conflicts. Make an active effort to involve all participants and listen to what they say. Summarize decisions as you go, clarifying action points and delivery deadlines at the end. Make sure everyone leaves the meeting aware of their action points. Circulate minutes promptly, not later than four days after the meeting. Request feedback from participants to involve them in the process.

The Meeting Process

Begins
Starts on time, without delays for latecomers

⇩

Works through a prepared agenda, in sequence, point by point

⇩

Summarizes the points made, and the decisions arising from the discussion

⇩

Ends
With a clear statement of action, and the schedule on which it must be achieved

Confident Team Management

At different stages in your working life, your role within a team will also vary. You may have to participate in, build, motivate, or lead a team. To succeed as a leader, you need to understand what makes a good team.

Handling Your Team

A team is a collection of people, but a group of people is not always a team. They become an effective force when united by a common objective, the same shared vision, and a confident leader at the helm, whose role is to ensure an understanding of, and enthusiasm for, the chosen strategy among all the team members.

It is important to monitor and review the progress being made by your team. You need to be on top of their needs; you may have to identify and put in place any necessary extra support. Liaison with other teams or within the company, including reporting on progress, is also part of the role. Get to know your team, their individual strengths and weaknesses, and how they work

Build a Strong Team Think of each team member's strengths as an asset to the whole, rather than concentrating too much on them individually.

Be an Effective Team Leader

Identify and agree on the strategy and vision with the team, but delegate implementation of the detail to team members.

→ Be confident; if you don't feel confident, appear so
→ Be reliable and consistent
→ Take responsibility
→ Focus on priorities and monitor progress
→ Develop listening and communication skills

→ Demonstrate drive and communicate urgency
→ Be flexible
→ Inspire your team, rather than instructing it
→ Use creative brainstorming to develop new ideas and approaches

together. Delegate the right task to the right person. Effective communication between you and your team is key, but equally important is positive communication between members themselves. You need to spot areas of potential friction or clashes of personality. Encourage contributions from all members, and deliver feedback, together with any necessary criticism, constructively.

Assemble an Effective Team

Assembling the right team is vital to the achievement of specific goals. It is important to identify and match individual team members' skills to the task, and to ensure a diversity of skills. Four accountants, one production manager, and one creative person for an advertising project, for example, would not be a sufficiently diverse mix. Management consultants maintain that four behavioral characteristics are required for team success: analysis, creativity, drive, and harmony. Once assembled, trust your team. Have confidence in your choice and their skills, and they will have confidence in you.

Present with Confidence

Presentations can sap your confidence, but preparation, practice, and constructive feedback will help you to become an effective, even a memorable, presenter.

Think around Your Subject

It may seem obvious, but a presentation needs a message. Establish the point of your presentation in your mind, then consider your potential audience. What level of knowledge of your subject will they have? How much explanation of the topic will you need to give? What are they expecting? How can you tailor your talk to the needs and interests of those attending? Will you need to persuade them of the value of your point?

Audience interest must be engaged, or it is lost

Check Your Props

Consider whether your presentation will be enhanced by the use of an overhead projector, PowerPoint, or other visual aids. Will they add to the message or simply make the delivery look slicker? It is a question of packaging versus content, and only you can make that choice.

think SMART

Instead of indulging your worries about your role as presenter, put yourself in your audience's place and ask what they would want you to tell them.

Thinking laterally serves a dual purpose:

- You will immediately start to feel less nervous.
- As you stop focusing on yourself, you will start to relax and be able to think more creatively about what would make your presentation appealing to the audience.

Eliminate Presentation Nerves

Most people will admit to suffering from presentation nerves at some point in their lives. The way to deal with them is to think of, and do, everything you can in advance to ensure your presentation's success—and then relax.

The audience is likely to be more understanding than you might think. Try to appear calm and confident, even if you are neither of these inside. The following tips will help:

→ Dress appropriately; consider wearing a bright jacket or tie, or adding accessories to help you to stand out.

→ Familiarize yourself with the room and its practicalities—equipment, lights, podium position, and sound system.

→ Practice deep breathing before the presentation to induce calm and improve your voice projection.

→ Try to relax, be yourself, and act naturally.

→ Begin with a well-prepared introduction and then follow a carefully planned but naturally flowing structure.

→ Show enthusiasm for your subject and enjoyment of the event—both are infectious.

Presentation Strategies

HIGH IMPACT

- Relaxing, being yourself, and acting naturally
- Addressing your audience in a friendly tone and taking time to establish a rapport
- Looking out at your audience as you talk
- Inviting feedback and encouraging a question-and-answer session

NEGATIVE IMPACT

- Taking on an adopted persona to present, to disguise nervousness
- Using a remote tone, without trying to engage with your audience
- Keeping your head down and reading from your notes
- Delivering your presentation like a lecture, rather than a chance to learn from one another

Start Your Own Business

Increased confidence will encourage you to take on bigger challenges. These could include a decision to set up on your own. You may feel that your potential can only be fulfilled by becoming your own boss.

Assess Your Idea

Naturally, you will need a business idea, but you will also need a vision for where you want to take it, and how to get there. Weigh up the advantages and disadvantages of going it alone. Take your time. You need to consider your decision; there is no need to leave your permanent job immediately. Seek professional advice, research your idea's potential, discuss it with contacts, and check out the competition, the market, and the funding options.

Analyze Your Idea

Research the unique selling point of your idea or product; how is it different, better, or unique?

⇩

Research potential customers for your product

⇩

Research competitors in your chosen sector

⇩

Research the size of the market, future trends, and their impact on your idea

Plan Your Moves

Time spent planning will pay huge dividends, and the knowledge that other people are in the same position is always reassuring when you're starting something new. Join the associations that will put you in touch with other business start-ups. You will learn about what support and funding is available, and you can exchange contacts. Other entrepreneurs can be a source of both comfort and inspiration. Talk to them about the pitfalls, and avoid falling into the same traps.

Ask What Makes an Entrepreneur

Ask yourself a few searching questions to see if you are a natural entrepreneur. Try to be truthful about your weaknesses as well as your strengths.

	Yes	No
Do I want to be in charge of my working life?	☐	☐
Do I long to put my personal stamp on a product or service?	☐	☐
Can I sell my business idea enthusiastically?	☐	☐
Can I handle rejection?	☐	☐
Am I prepared to work long, unsociable hours?	☐	☐
Am I prepared to cut back financially if necessary?	☐	☐
Am I prepared to be customer-focused?	☐	☐
Is security low-priority for me as a motivator?	☐	☐
Is my family supportive of my decision?	☐	☐
Can I handle the bad times with the good?	☐	☐

Do You Enjoy Risk? To make it as an entrepreneur you need to feel challenged by risk rather than afraid of it. If you answered "Yes" to the majority of the questions in the list above, you may have what it takes to go it alone.

> **There are those who look at things the way they are, and ask why; I dream of things that never were, and ask why not.**
>
> Robert F. Kennedy

5

Your Confident Future

When you are inspired by a book or a course, you usually remain on a high for a few days. Then your routine intervenes. Your immediate surroundings—people, work, and life—remain the same, and your energy and determination to change fade, despite your good intentions. This final chapter will show you how to:

- Sustain and develop change
- Explore your goals and make them happen
- Find ways to become more energetic
- Surround yourself with supportive people
- Visualize success in ways that work

Change Your Habits

If you can change even a tiny aspect of your life, it will make you feel in charge—and small changes can pave the way for bigger ones. Confident people approach change with optimism rather than seeing it as a threat.

Get Results Fast

Change may take more effort than you think, but it can take surprisingly little time. Time-management experts maintain that it takes only three weeks to replace an old habit with a new behavior, and only another nine weeks for that behavior to become a habit itself. For example, maybe your biggest confidence block is your shyness. If you make it a rule to talk with one new person every day, however small those encounters are, after three weeks you will find that meeting new people is already less of an ordeal. Step up the rule slightly and ask yourself to attend one social function every week and talk to someone new in that context. If you do this even one week in two over

CASE study: Making Success a Habit

Sasha, an advertising executive, hated presenting to clients. He could handle groups of two or three people well, but with a larger audience he lost his fluency and became wooden. His manager suggested that he go on a course to improve his presenting skills. Its results were immediate: he presented much more smoothly.

Then, in one big presentation, a difficult client challenged him with a sequence of aggressive questions. Sasha stumbled slightly, and the client persisted; eventually, Sasha recalled the skills he'd learned and answered the questions. Although there were some awkward pauses, he continued and completed his presentation.

• *Despite his momentary loss of confidence, Sasha had acquired the habit of presenting successfully, and could call on it when his confidence slipped.*
• *Sasha also learned that, however well you are handling a situation, you are only in charge of your own behavior, not anyone else's.*

the next nine weeks, you've worked your way into a new habit. If you have been shy for 30 years, just 12 weeks to break the habit of a lifetime is a quick result.

Choose Where to Start

If there are a lot of areas in your life you would like to change, you may wonder where to start. Sort out your priorities to ensure success:

- Start with something achievable. If you find it difficult to present at meetings, choose a small, unimportant one to practice change. Don't make a radical decision to begin to change at the largest meeting that the whole company attends. You can work up to it.

It is simpler to start with small changes than large ones

- Choose a skill that will make a difference. Make sure you work on things that are worth working on. Perhaps learning problem-solving techniques might be the skill that will distinguish your team at work from the rest? You need a clear, desirable goal to motivate change.

Persist with Change

Only work on one or two issues at a time. Even if you want to make many changes, working toward too many goals will confuse you. Decide on the changes you want most and work with those first. Remember, too, that the key to change is persistence. Keep practicing until change seems natural. At first, you will be familiarizing yourself with the process of change as much as you are working toward a goal, but as you become used to the idea of change, and have effected some changes, you can broaden your goals.

TIP Use setbacks to build your strength. The more setbacks you overcome, the more firmly grounded your confidence will be.

Explore Your Goals

Having goals is an essential part of motivation for the future. Keep them flexible, though; you may reach them more quickly than you thought, or more slowly. You may even decide to change them altogether.

Organize Your Goals

When goals remain nebulous, it is usually because of a thinking pattern that blocks you from taking the next step. If, for example, you have always wanted to live and work in France, but have never taken the idea any further, ask yourself what is stopping you. You will probably find that an internal voice supplies the answer: it might say "I don't even speak French," "Jobs will be hard to find," or, pushing the goal farther away, "That's just a dream; there's no way I could realize it." These difficulties aren't real, because you have never done the research to back them up. The way to overcome them is to break the goal into manageable components, and then look at each component carefully. But if you take no action, your voices will be right—you won't have expended any effort, but you won't have achieved anything, either.

Only action can make goals happen

think SMART

If you are thinking, "I can't do that," step out of character and think of someone else saying it.

- Imagine your best friend telling you that you will fail.
- Tell them why they are wrong, and why you will succeed.
- A short mental argument with negativity will help to stop you from sabotaging yourself.

Change Your Goals

As your thinking becomes more agile and flexible, you may find that your goals move further, become more ambitious, or change altogether. Don't feel that you need to stick through thick and thin to a goal you once held, even if everything else has changed. Greater self-knowledge may reveal that a goal was a daydream and that you are actually happier either keeping it as one, without putting effort and research into turning it into reality, or dismissing it altogether.

Keep Your Goals Visible

Write your goals down. In the forest of details that makes up everyday life, you tend to forget what you promised yourself, and your true wishes get obscured by trivial things that really matter much less. Keep your goals handy—on your nightstand, stuck on refrigerator, written in a diary—and look at them every week. Ask yourself whether they are staying static, if they are getting closer, or if they are changing. Goals left unchallenged petrify into unrealizable dreams. Your goals need to be current, relevant, and achievable.

The Path to Change

You have always dreamed of living in France

Find out about the possibility of jobs in France in your field

Start taking French classes in the evenings

Go to France for a week to see the area in which you might be working

Look at your goal again and see how much closer it has moved

Find Your Energizers

Low energy is often a sign that you aren't happy with your surroundings. Look for the situations and people that give you energy, register what their special qualities are, then look for more of them.

Be an Energizer

Everyone has suffered from the moaning acquaintance: the one with whom you dread getting trapped on the telephone. They have a litany of things that have gone wrong, and just a short conversation leaves you feeling drained. Ask yourself if you ever play the same part. It's natural to feel discontented sometimes, but it's a bad habit to get into. Other people will avoid you because you sap their energy, and you'll find it hard to refuel on your own. If you catch yourself moaning, pull the conversation up short and set it going on a more positive note. Ask a friend to tell you if you're being negative. Even if you don't feel like an energizer inside, you can behave like one.

Energizers Vary At some times, a day with your family may reenergize you; at others, you may want a stimulating chat or debate with a colleague.

TECHNIQUES
to practice

Practice playing the part of an energizer. If you look and behave like someone positive and energetic, other people will respond well to you and help the role-playing to become reality.

From today, learn to like yourself more. Sell yourself to yourself:

1 Stand in front of a full-length mirror. Look carefully at how you are standing.

2 Imagine a cord through your spine, pulling you upward like a puppet. Square your shoulders and stand straight and relaxed.

3 Pay attention to your breathing. Breathe in slowly, counting to five. Breathe out to the same count.

4 Mentally count five things that you are looking forward to about today.

5 Meet your own gaze in the mirror and smile. Ask yourself if you look like someone you'd enjoy talking to.

If the answer isn't positive yet, repeat the exercise until you look outgoing, welcoming, and relaxed. Run through the steps again in your head at various points in the day.

Find Other Energizers

Energetic people project outward rather than turning inward. They confidently make sure that their needs are met, and then look at what they can do with and for other people. Forge links with other energizers by recognizing their qualities and showing an immediate interest in them. If you're shy, use the FORE technique to get a conversation going, and make sure that you listen as much as you talk. Dismiss any of your old confidence-sapping gremlins asking "Why would someone happy and successful like that bother with me?"

They will bother with you because you are energetic, interesting, and confident—in short, because you are worth bothering with.

> **Failure is more frequently from want of energy than want of capital.**
>
> Daniel Webster

Use Encouragement and Support

When you lack confidence, you tend to lean on supportive friends and colleagues. As your confidence grows, you will find that support acts as a springboard to propel you to greater achievements and successes.

Find the Right Encouragement

Confident people tend to have wider support groups, as they make connections more easily than the less confident You have already chosen your Secret Service group to give you feedback about your strengths and work performance To keep your confidence-building program going and to use it to help you achieve your goals, you will need either to use the same people, or to establish a wider group who will reward, encourage, and sustain you as you change. Don't confuse sympathy with support, however. The two aren't mutually exclusive, and sympathy can be enjoyable if you aren't very confident: you recount a situation in which you came out the worst, and your friend or colleague offers a "poor you" response. In the short term this may make you feel better, but it does nothing to get you out of a victim mind-set, and it won't challenge you or help you become more self-reliant in the long term. Move outside your comfort zone as your confidence increases, step by step, and look for friends who will make positive suggestions and support change, rather than those who will simply offer an emotional crutch.

Getting Support from Friends

HIGH IMPACT

- Making active, positive suggestions for change
- Helping you to look forward to a successful future
- Restating the positive things about your situation

NEGATIVE IMPACT

- Sympathizing without any positive input
- Dwelling with you on negative events on the past
- Reinforcing a passive, "life is tough" mind-set

Use Physical Activity

Physical activity helps you to think optimistically and positively. If possible, part of your program should

Fulfill Both Criteria Physical activity is mentally refreshing, and so is the company of supportive friends. Find some time to combine the two.

incorporate a sport or other physical activity. Even if—perhaps especially if—you are not a very active type, and have a built-in resistance to organized sports or games, search out some kind of exercise that you can enjoy with friends or colleagues. You don't necessarily have to join your local softball team; bowling or regular walks in the country with like-minded people will have a similar effect, raising your endorphin levels and your spirits, and helping you to broaden your outlook.

TIP Finding the right kind of support is as important as getting enough of it.

Learn to Face Forward

You've embarked on your journey and effected some changes. As your confidence grows, your outlook broadens, too. It's time to imagine how some of those long-term goals will feel when you reach them.

Work with Yourself

Just because you are trying to challenge yourself doesn't mean that you can't work in a way that comes naturally to you. As you create action plans for the future, think about how you have learned best in the past and what has already worked well for you. Work with your strengths, rather than against them: some people may want to research around a goal before committing themselves to a course of action, others may want guidance from a life coach or other specialist; still others may prefer to go it alone, but with regular feedback sessions from friends or colleagues. Work out a plan that suits you—one that includes short-term, medium-term and long-term goals—and a way of working that suits you, and then stick to it.

> **As you climb the mountain, remember to enjoy the scenery**

Enjoy the Journey

Take time to relish successes on the way to reaching your goals. Concentrate on the desired end result—but not so hard that you forget to enjoy the process of reaching it. If your end goal is a promotion at work, for example, appreciate the small steps that will get you there (a well-received presentation; a compliment from the CEO) in their own right, not just as building blocks to your end goal. Extra confidence helps you to enjoy life to the fullest, so take advantage of your growing skills as you require them. Above all, look to the future with open, optimistic vision, and always imagine that it will be even better than the present.

Visualize Your Success

In order to focus on your future, you need a vision of the changed you at the front of your mind. Visualization helps to build a bridge between you and the future, and allows you to think and feel positively about the change.

First, you need to relax:
→ Sit on a comfortable chair or lie down on a bed, supporting your head with a pillow.
→ Take a deep breath and exhale slowly; repeat.
→ Tense and relax each set of muscles in your body separately (arms and hands, shoulders, neck, face, stomach, thighs
→ As you breath out, let your body become heavier and heavier, and more and more relaxed.

When you are completely relaxed, imagine that you are the star in your own movie. Visualize yourself as vividly as possible. Turn the controls up on your imaginary screen to get the maximum definition and color.
→ Imagine the old you, doing all the things you would be doing and saying.

Watch yourself for a moment. Now erect a new screen. You are looking at the new you, at how you want to be. Ask yourself
→ What would you be doing?
→ Who would you be with?
→ How would you look, and how would you feel?

Watch the image enlarge itself and move off toward the future horizon. Tell yourself "this is how I will be," and believe that it will happen. Waken yourself slowly and repeat the exercise every night before going to sleep.

> **The best choice, for each individual, is the highest it is possible for him to achieve.**
>
> Aristotle

Index

Picture Credits

The publisher would like to thank the following for their kind permission to reproduce their photographs: Abbreviations key : (l) = left, (c) = center, (r) = right, (t) = top, (b) = below, (cl) = center left, (cr) = center right.

1: Holger Winkler/zefa/Corbis (l), Reg Charity/Corbis (c), Stephen Toner/Getty (r); **2:** Johannes Kroemer/Getty; **3:** Adrian Turner (t), Creatas/Photolibrary.com (c), Adrian Turner (b); **5:** Peter Cade/Iconica/Getty; **7:** Eric Wessman/Iconica/Getty; **8:** Alt-6 / Alamy (l), Ericka McConnell/The Image Bank/Getty (cl), Ghislain and Marie David de Lossy/Getty (cr), Jim Craigmyle/Corbis (r); **13:** Imagestate; **17:** Randy Faris/Corbis; **21:** Adrian Turner; **23:** Ericka McConnell/The Image Bank/Getty; **27:** Creatas/Photolibrary.com; **28:** Holger Winkler/zefa/Corbis; **33:** Rommel/Masterfile; **37:** Adrian Weinbrecht/Taxi/Getty; **55:** Matthias Clamer/Getty; **57:** Comstock Premium/Alamy; **67:** Brad Wilson/Iconica/Getty; **69:** Butch Martin/Getty; **73:** Chabruken/Taxi/Getty; **75:** Stephen Toner/Stone/Getty; **87:** Reg Charity/Corbis; **93:** Ghislain & Marie David de Lossy/Getty; **97:** Chuck Elliott/The Image Bank/Getty; **101:** Adrian Turner; **106:** Jim Craigmyle/Corbis; **109:** Eric Wessman/Iconica/Getty; **111:** Colin Hawkins/Getty.

All other images © Dorling Kindersley.

For further information see www.dkimages.com

Acknowledgments

Two books were particularly helpful in researching this title, the *Mind Map Handbook*, by Tony Buzan (Thorsons, 2005) and *The One*, by William F. Harley Jr. (Fleming H. Revell, 2002).

Author's Biography

ROS TAYLOR worked as a senior clinical psychologist in the UK National Health Service before moving to business in 1981. Ros broadcasts regularly on television and radio and has recently completed two books to accompany her BBC2 documentary series Confidence Lab. Ros has been described by the *Independent on Sunday* as one of the ten top life coaches in Britain.